MARATHON QUEST

The final, 250th marathon, Cochrane, Alberta.

MARATHON QUEST

MARTIN PARNELL

RMB

Victoria Vancouver Calgary

Rocky Mountain Books
www.rmbooks.com

Library and Archives Canada Cataloguing in Publication
Parnell, Martin
Marathon quest / Martin Parnell.
Includes index.
Issued also in electronic formats.
ISBN 978-1-927330-14-2 (HTML).—ISBN 978-1-927330-33-3 (PDF)
ISBN 978-1-927330-13-5 (pbk.)

1. Parnell, Martin. 2. Athletes—Alberta—Biography. 3. Philanthropists—
Alberta—Biography. 4. Sports—Social aspects. 5. Marathon running.
6. Physical education and training. 7. Nutrition. I. Title.

GV697.P37A3 2012   796.092   C2012-903844-X

Front cover photo: Tobi McLeod
Printed in Canada

Rocky Mountain Books acknowledges the financial support for its publishing
program from the Government of Canada through the Canada Book Fund (CBF)
and the Canada Council for the Arts, and from the province of British Columbia
through the British Columbia Arts Council and the Book Publishing Tax Credit.

 Canadian Heritage   Patrimoine canadien   Canada Council for the Arts   Conseil des Arts du Canada

 BRITISH COLUMBIA ARTS COUNCIL
Supported by the Province of British Columbia

This book was produced using FSC®-certified, acid-free paper,
processed chlorine free and printed with vegetable-based inks.

 MIX
Paper from responsible sources
FSC® C016245

For Sue, who was with me every step of the way.

Whatever you can do, or dream you can do, begin it.
Boldness has genius, power, and magic in it!
　　　　　　　—GOETHE, "Prelude at the Theatre," *Faust*,
　　　　　　　free translation by John Anster, 1835

We don't stop playing because we grow old;
we grow old because we stop playing.
　　　　　　　—JOSEPH LEE (1862–1937),
　　　　　　　Father of the American Playground Movement

Contents

Foreword   9

Preface   11

1   Starting Out   17
2   Learning to Run   25
3   Running West: From Marathons to Triathlons   35
4   Tour d'Afrique: An Epiphany   43
5   Almost an Ironman   65
6   Moving up to Ultras   73
7   Right To Play   81
8   Winter: Now That's Cold   97
9   Spring: Not with a Bang, but a Whimper   113
10   Summer: Highs and Lows   131
11   Autumn: Out of the Darkness and Into the Light   139
12   Winter Again: The Quest Comes to a Close   157
13   Cool Down, Check In, Then Comrades   171
14   And on to Benin   187

Afterword   199

Acknowledgements   207

Riding the open road in Tanzania.

Foreword

The idea of play is not about age, gender or physical ability. It is, in Martin Parnell's words, "about allowing a person to grow, change and become stronger." *Marathon Quest* recounts Martin's incredible journey of running 250 marathons in 2010 in support of Right To Play, and how he was able to touch the lives of thousands of children and adults across the world.

Throughout the book, Parnell exemplifies the extraordinary impact that sport and play can have, no matter your age or ability. *Marathon Quest* is about Martin's relationship with play through running: why he started, how it helped him through challenges, and how it allowed him to engage with the world in a new and inspiring way. He shares his journey of overcoming the physical and mental barriers that were preventing him from growing and changing, what compelled him to complete so many marathons in a single year, and why he chose to support Right To Play. Although we came from very different places and starting points, the parallels between Parnell's journey and mine are remarkable.

For me, the 1994 Lillehammer Olympics developed into something more than winning medals. Like Parnell's experiences while cycling the Tour d'Afrique, the people I met in Eritrea before the 1994 Olympics touched me deeply and changed the course of my life forever. This experience was something greater than creating change; it was about transforming lives through the power of play.

Parnell experienced first-hand how play encourages reconciliation and leadership through team-building exercises, increases self-confidence by providing those who had been silenced a voice, and builds enthusiasm and motivation to realize their full potential. But most importantly, play provides children with alternatives to crime and self-destructive behaviours by giving them a safe space to play.

When Martin Parnell approached Right To Play with the Marathon Quest 250 proposal in 2009, we were all extremely excited, but could not have imagined the impact Martin would have on Right To Play or the friendship that has blossomed with this inspirational man. Throughout the book, Martin exemplifies the spirit of Right To Play in every aspect of his journey, beginning with an unenthusiastic middle school teacher, all the way to the moment he crossed the finish line on December 31, 2010. The challenges Martin Parnell has overcome exemplifies his strength of character and passion. He is extraordinary in his ability to adapt to situations, to continue despite all odds, to address challenges as they arise and persevere through pain, and to see beyond immediate challenges and find joy in everything he does. His passion and drive put him in the same class as some of the world's greatest athletes.

Marathon Quest is about more than running and racing. It's about testing limits, overcoming challenges and recognizing the power of community. Martin Parnell's story embodies inclusiveness: while he shares his individual journey, he is quick to mention that he could not have succeeded without the love and support from the people in his life and those he met along the way. Parnell's connection with Right To Play runs much deeper than dollars and fundraising. Like the Right To Play Red Ball, Parnell is a symbol for the power an individual can have in inspiring and mobilizing a community. His story is a testament to how sport and play can encourage change for the better. It is a privilege and a joy to have met this extraordinary man and to have him support Right To Play wholeheartedly. I would like to sincerely thank Martin Parnell for everything he has done to support Right To Play in the past and for everything he does in the future. I wish him all the best in every adventure he chooses to undertake.

–Johann Olav Koss,
President and CEO,
Right To Play

Preface

LAST MARATHON

*"Begin at the beginning and go on until
you come to the end and then stop."*
—LEWIS CARROLL, *Alice in Wonderland*

Friday, December 31, 2010

I open my eyes and it's pitch black. I close them again and it's still pitch black. In the dark, I listen: Is the wind howling? Is snow or sleet hammering against the window? What time is it? I grab my Garmin FR60 race watch from the bedside table – it measures everything. My heart rate, speed, distance, number of steps taken. My watch knows that I've completed 12,927,214 steps over the course of the year, and today, the final day, I will take another 51,000.

I find the light button on the Garmin and a blue glow highlights the numbers: 5:14 a.m. Time to do a check-up on this 55-year-old body, as I've done 249 times this year. I have a list: feet, good; ankles, good; calves, tight but no cramping. This morning they are sound, much better than they felt after Marathon 028 back in late February, when my left shin had swollen to twice its normal size, and I had to stop running for two and a half weeks. Next, the knees, quads and hamstrings: check, check and check. Finally, the glutes and back: both are fine this morning. I had problems all summer with the sciatic nerve in my glutes, though. I tried active release therapy, physiotherapy, Ibuprofen, muscle relaxants and stretching. Nothing worked. In desperation, I asked my physiotherapist, Serge, what to do. He suggested acupuncture. After two sessions of needles in my butt, the pain went away.

Thankful for the seemingly small gift of a pain-free body, I crawl out of bed at 5:30 and throw on a pair of shorts. I peek between the curtains and see an icy mist rolling down the river. Not good. Sue is still sleeping, and so, with a sigh, I go into the guest bathroom to splash some water on my face.

Four years ago, Sue decided that instead of asking our guests to sign a guest book, we would invite them to write on this washroom wall. As I carry out my morning routine, I read: "Your mind is like a parachute. It won't work unless it's open," and "Today is a gift – that's why we call it the present." Someone's written: "'Trying is the first step towards failure.' –Homer Simpson." Good one. The pièce de résistance in the throne room, however, is my marathon calendar.

Sue has marked the marathons in groups of five, and every day after I finish I cross one off. These markings tell the story of the year. The injuries are listed: damaged left shin (Marathon 028); pinched nerve in back (057); fell over (104, 134, 135). As well, we've listed the official races I've undertaken: Boston, Vancouver, Red Deer, Calgary, Regina, Victoria, Las Vegas. Two hundred forty-nine days are crossed off, only one lonely soldier left. Today, I aim to cross him off too.

It's time to put a number to the weather. I shuffle to the front door – my joints are still warming up – and I check the thermometer outside: −27°c. Could be worse, and it has been. On January 1, 2010, when I started Marathon Quest 250, it was −32! I waddle back to the bedroom and choose my outfit for the day. If it were −5°, I would only need one layer on the bottom and three on top. At −20, I've found it advisable to wear two layers below and four on top. Today I'll start with three layers on the bottom and five on top. I can strip down as the day wears on.

I continue with my usual routine. Breakfast is the same every day, no variation and why not? I love it: Mini-Wheats, Almond Crunch, plain yogourt, strawberries, blueberries, blackberries, a banana, milk and coffee for a caffeine kick. To complete my marathons, I needed to pay attention to nutrition. It's not complicated, but it is critical.

First of all, I needed to ensure I ate 5,000 calories or more per day. Then I had to ensure I was getting what I needed during the run. There are three components to on-the-run nutrition: water (hydration), calories (fuel) and electrolytes (salt). Paying heed to this trinity of elements, each marathon morning for the past year, I've prepared my hydration pack for the 42.2 km ahead of me. Today's routine is no different. My CamelBak hydration pack holds 3 litres of liquid. My fuel is Carbo-Pro, which I mix with water, allowing me an intake of 300 calories an hour for every half-litre I drink. I also carry 12 Thermolyte Metasalt capsules for added electrolytes; after the first half-hour of a run, I take two and then two more every hour. Other items in my pack include an emergency rain jacket (garbage bag), toilet paper, two sweet-and-salty chewy bars, my cell phone, camera and IMP, a *Star Wars* imperial storm trooper figure I found in the gravel at a gas station. He's my lucky mascot and has been to all the big races.

IMP, an Imperial Storm Trooper, waits at Hopkinton before the start of the 2010 Boston Marathon.

I have another cup of coffee. It's 7:45 and I have to leave in 15 minutes. I'm trying not to think too much about the coming day. I know I'm going to be a mess by 3:00 p.m. To distract myself, I click onto the Marathon Quest website and check out how the fundraising is going. I had wanted to raise $250,000 by now, but it's not going to happen. The donation thermometer tells me we're at $190,801.50. I should be thrilled, but I'm not. My objective has been to raise money for the kids, for an amazing international humanitarian organization called Right To Play (RTP).

Right To Play helps create social change in 20 countries around the world – including North America – that are affected by disease, poverty and war. It brings sport and play – through programs, events and festivals – to children who may not otherwise have access to organized play or coaches. The games and programs Right To Play brings to these children are developmental: on-the-ground coaches and volunteers engage kids and help them learn. They encourage children to be active community members, help them grow to be self-actualized individuals and instruments of social change. Former child soldiers, marginalized girls, refugees and kids affected by disabilities, HIV and AIDS, have all benefited from the programs Right To Play sponsors in countries as far apart as Benin and South Sudan, Mali and China.

Over the past few years, RTP's mandate and my personal goals have found common ground in ways I could never have imagined until perhaps this moment. Running changed my life, pulled me up from a low place and into the light, allowing me not only to move forward but also to become this person I am today, at this age I am today. And by "becoming" myself, I have been able to use my strength to help others. Sport has changed my life, just as it has helped thousands of RTP's participants. I do believe that "play" can change the world, one person at a time. Whether you rediscover play at age 47, when I started running, or at 7, 27, 67 or 87, it opens your eyes to the world, your family and your community.

Fifty dollars funds a child with a Right To Play program for one year. When I started Marathon Quest (MQ) 250, I made a commitment to provide programs for 5,000 kids.

This morning, I am disappointed that I'm not making my goal, but what can I do? I've got some control over the running and how I convey the message to my audience, but I have no control over who gives when and how much. I wonder why people can't see what I see when I consider all the good work RTP does. I quickly realize I can't dwell on this. I have to go out and finish the job.

As I shut down the computer, Sue is packing a bag. It contains a Right To Play banner, MQ 250 pamphlets and posters. All through the year Sue's been packing bags: luggage for the next race, extra clothes bags. She has been steadfast from the beginning of this adventure. When I first told her I wanted to run 365 marathons in a year, she sent me to see the doctor. With the advice of Dr. Hanlon, I whittled that number down to 250: five a week. In committing to tackling this crazy year of marathons, I had essentially told Sue I was putting my life on hold for a year, and she promised to support me. I couldn't have got through the year without her.

Well, I'm ready. There's no turning back. Today's route is a little different than the one I've been hammering out over the past year. I'll be running at the Spray Lake Sawmills Family Sport Centre, starting at 9:00 a.m. and finishing at 3:00 p.m. Yes, the finish, the final 42.2 km of the 10,550 km. I know I'm tired. I love running, but I'm ready to take it down a notch.

Sue drives me down to the sport centre, arriving at 8:00. I meet Robin, the centre's facility manager. A grader is trying to sort out the section of the route that crosses over to the already cleared pathways. The centre is a hub of activity. Mark from Trailblazers Camping & Outdoor store is setting up the raffle stall and Bobbi has collected the necessary two vats of Tim Horton's coffee and hot chocolate. Sue and I hang around chatting with small groups of runners. Soon we head outside, and by 9:00 a.m. 30 runners are there, ready to join me on the last marathon. I count down from ten to one, and then I blow my bear whistle.

As a group, we face forward and take the first steps of the last marathon. As an individual, I reflect on the events that have brought me to this point.

1
STARTING OUT

"Families are like fudge – mostly sweet with a few nuts."
—ANONYMOUS

Many athletes will tell you they have always been athletic, were always picked first for teams on the playground, always had a desire to run or shoot hoops or slap a puck into the net. Some will say they were always focused on their sport, that it was their one true calling and goal. I had a different lead-up to my running "career," and I came to running relatively late in life. But when I think about my beginnings, I realize that all of my early experiences and running idols helped point me in a certain direction, if perhaps in a roundabout way.

I have always been told I was a "huggable" baby. That meant I had fat cheeks and ample baby fat. The fat cheeks were always getting pinched by aunts and grandmothers. I was born in 1955 in Buckfastleigh, Devon, England, the eldest of six kids, including Sally, Jan, Louise, Peter and Andrew.

When I was 11 my family almost emigrated to Australia, but bought my grandmother's rundown 13th-century farmhouse instead. Mum and Dad worked hard to turn it into a guest house, and we kids helped. At around this time I moved up to grammar school: a new level of education, a new level of teasing, thanks to my persistent baby fat. Because I was a "good size," I was picked to play Number 8 on the rugby team. This is the person who holds the scrum together at the back and gets his ears rubbed off.

When I was 14 I took a hiatus from rugby, and school, for about eight weeks, after the doctor diagnosed me with rheumatic fever. I had to stay in bed at home and not move. It wasn't all bad, as Mum bought me bunches of grapes, and I watched every episode

Me in my very smart St Joseph's School uniform.

of *A Man Called Ironside*. I also immersed myself in comics. My favourite character was Alf Tupper, a fictional, working-class, hard-as-nails runner whose adventures under the title *Tough of the Track* appeared first in *The Rover* and then *The Victor*, British boys' comics.

Alf's most endearing characteristic was his love of fish and chips, and he won many a race and rescued many a citizen in distress, sustained by the stuff. He worked as a welder and was the eternal underdog. He had many obstacles to overcome, but he usually came through in the end. What a guy!

After the summer holiday, I was back at school but was told to keep away from sports. But by the spring of the next year, the doctor said I was making good progress and could start getting some exercise. Finally, by the next fall, I felt I was well enough to take a few more steps forward. I asked the sports teacher if I could compete in the one-mile race at the school sports day. He wasn't enthusiastic but said yes. My first experience with running would be quite an event.

The race was four times around the course. The gun went off and I hammered around the track. Then I saw the sports teacher waving frantically at me to come off. I pulled off and asked, "What's wrong?"

"Your face is beet red, and I was worried you were going to collapse."

So ended my running career – for the time being.

During my 16th year I grew six inches, which caused some upset and confusion when my peers had to find a replacement nickname for me. By the end of the spurt, I was no longer "Tubby Parnell" but "Bean Pole Parnell." (There was a period of three days while I was growing when nobody called me anything. You can't win.) In the meantime, it was time for me to make a choice between arts and sciences. I chose maths, physics and economics as I was thinking of pursuing a career in engineering, mostly because I wanted to travel, make good money and not have to wear a tie.

In the end, I chose to become a mining engineer and trained at the Camborne School of Mines. During the summers, I worked at two mines, one a fluorspar mine in County Durham for ICI and the other an open-pit lead and zinc mine for Cominco Ltd. at Pine Point along Great Slave Lake in Canada's Northwest Territories. When I graduated I really wanted to return to Canada, but the major employers in 1976 were in Zambia and South Africa. However, I was intent on the Great White North, so I wrote to my former boss at Pine Point and asked if there were any engineer-in-training opportunities available with Cominco. There were, if I could get my landed immigrant status sorted out. I thought I would be posted to Yellowknife, but I ended up in Kimberley, BC, at the underground lead-zinc Sullivan Mine.

On August 19, 1977, at the age of 22, I left England. It was a foggy day and Mum and Dad drove me up to London, Heathrow. I had bought a backpack and filled it with all my worldly goods. I had sixty dollars in my pocket, which was enough to get from the airport to a hotel in Kimberley. When I arrived, I soon found an apartment near the mine offices and set to work as engineer-in-training, planning the mining of ore blocks. My boss at the mine was Tom, an Aussie for whom I had a lot of respect – we got along well. Little did I realize the impact he would have on my life 35 years later.

During my two years in that beautiful Rocky Mountain town, I worked hard, refined my skiing skills and made forays in society. I even broke into a sports club where I decided to try out that most Canadian of sports, hockey. Before taking up with a recreational league, I had only ice skated once, in Bristol, where I had wobbled around the rink about ten times (clutching the boards all the way) before going for a cup of tea. By the end of my time with recreational hockey in Kimberley, I wasn't the best skater but I could pick up a pass and feed it off.

By June 1979, Cominco had decided I should go to Yellowknife after all, and I started at the Con gold mine in August. I joined a local hockey team, The Dusters, which was made up mostly of teachers from the local schools. One of those, a physical education teacher at St. Patrick's School, Gerard, is, to this day, one of my best friends. We were both keen to improve our social lives. We took part in various sports activities and even joined a dance group. Gerard tells hilarious stories about our activities as we prepared for a dance performance.

Gerard's teacher friends were always trying to match him up with single women teachers, one of whom was a very attractive brunette named Wendy. However, as fate would have it, it was me she ended up falling in love with, and I felt the same about her. Happily, she agreed to be my wife.

These were high times for me in Yellowknife. Not only had I found someone I would soon marry, but in the summer of 1980 I experienced something that I'd never seen before, something that has stuck with me until this day and continues to inspire me.

During that summer, I began hearing stories of a young man who was trying to run across Canada to raise money for cancer research. His name was Terry Fox, and his quest was called the Marathon of Hope. What made Terry's goal so remarkable was that he had had one of his legs amputated due to cancer, so he ran with a prosthetic leg. Terry had started his ultramarathon in early April from St. John's, Newfoundland. On September 1 he was forced to stop just outside of Thunder Bay, Ontario. Canadians were compelled by his story, by his desire to run, to change the world. Every year, communities small and large still hold Terry Fox Runs to raise money for cancer research. In September 1982 Gerard and I joined in and raised funds for the Terry Fox Foundation by running the 10 km event. As touched as I was by Terry's work, I could not have guessed how his endeavour would stay with me, and how it would contribute to my own life, so many years later.

Wendy and I married in 1983 and relocated briefly to Pine Point, where I was to work as production engineer at the same mine I had previously been employed at. Wendy found work at a local school.

CLIFF YOUNG

In 1983 Cliff Young, an unknown potato farmer, ran Australia's ultra-tough 875 km endurance race from Sydney to Melbourne. Usually the race was run by athletes who trained long and hard for the ordeal. Cliff showed up, took his number and explained to curious media reporters that his training came from rounding up sheep on foot, sometimes running for three days in a row over the 810 hectares of his family's ranch. He figured he could run the race.

Some were skeptical, especially when they saw the way Cliff ran: shuffling along like an old man. The pack was ahead of him at first. But, while the others took six hours to sleep before they started running for the day, Cliff didn't stop. He didn't know he was supposed to sleep, and slowly he inched ahead, eventually passing the pack of athletes. By the last day he was well in the lead.

Cliff won the race and broke the record by nine hours; he finished in five days, 15 hours and four minutes. He was an instant hero. His distinctive shuffle-run is now called the Young, or Cliffy, Shuffle, and endurance racers have adopted his technique.

My young cousin, Mary, fell in love with Cliff as she watched him run and win the race and then give his prize money to five other runners. She said to her mother, "I'm going to marry that man." And she did.

After a year, however, we decided to take some time off to travel. We visited my parents in England and toured Europe in a vw camper. Then, in 1985, we set out to explore India, Thailand and Australia. I now realize how fortunate it was that we decided to make this trip while we were young, rather than put it off until we retired.

I have quite a few aunts, uncles and cousins on Australia's east coast, and Wendy and I spent some time with them. One of my aunts, Theresa, lived in Indented Head, Victoria. Her 23-year-old daughter, Mary, was at the time married to Australian runner Cliff Young, who, at age 63, was an ultramarathon icon. I found myself in the presence of a runner who would spring to mind later in my life and help me to persevere. When I met Mary and Cliff in April 1985, Cliff was getting ready to run the Sydney–Melbourne race again. During Marathon Quest 250, I thought of Cliff many times as I used the "Cliffy Shuffle" to get me through a number of tough days.

When Wendy and I returned to Canada, we settled in Sudbury, Ontario, where I gained employment with Falconbridge as an equipment technologist, researching new mining equipment for the company's underground nickel–copper operations. Wendy began teaching with the Sudbury Catholic School Board and we began a wonderful life together. In 1989 we adopted two children, a little boy, Kyle, aged 4, and his 2-year-old sister, Kristina. Despite having a huge impact on our lives, they brought us much joy and now our family was complete.

I progressed from mine engineer to mine superintendent and eventually to manager of human resources. Wendy enjoyed her work as a teacher. We found a wonderful lady named Christena to look after the children while Wendy and I were at work. Kyle and Kristina adored her and her husband, Gordon, who became surrogate grandparents. Even though the children are grown and Kristina now has children of her own, we still regard Christena and Gordon as family.

All was well in our lives until June 2001, when everything came crashing down and our lives would change forever.

Wendy and I shared many common interests and one of them was dance. We weren't exactly Fred Astaire and Ginger Rogers, but we always enjoyed social occasions when we were given the opportunity to strut our stuff. In the summer of 2001 we found ourselves in just such a situation: we were attending a friend's wedding and were on the dance floor. As I held Wendy in my arms, she flinched and mentioned a pain in her side. We really thought nothing of it at the time, but after it persisted for a couple of weeks, Wendy went to the doctor. Tests followed, and in August we received the devastating news. My beloved wife Wendy was diagnosed with cancer of the liver. It was so unexpected; we never imagined that the diagnosis would be anything serious. After a very honest and heart-wrenching session with the consultant, Wendy turned to me and said, "I won't see Christmas." Her comment was prescient, and despite all our prayers and her very brave battle, my soulmate passed away on December 11 of that year.

The children and I were forced to face our loss and were left with no choice but to carry on, with a huge void in our lives.

2
LEARNING TO RUN

"Jogging is very beneficial. It's good for your legs and your feet. It's also very good for the ground. It makes it feel needed."
—CHARLES SCHULZ, *Peanuts*

Running wasn't something I naturally turned to as a way to find balance again after Wendy's passing. In fact, if it weren't for my brother Peter, I may not have started running and my life would now be very different. But because Peter issued a challenge to me and my other brother, Andy, I found myself trying to figure out how to "train." I had no idea how much I would like running and how much it would sustain me.

One year after Wendy's passing, I was still trying to put my life back together. It was at this time that I received a call from Peter. It may sound strange, but I didn't really know him very well. I had left England at the age of 18, when he was 10 and my other brother and youngest of the family, Andy, was only eight. Peter, along with his wife, Helen, had been police officers in London before emigrating to Canada in 2000 with their two boys, Jonathan and Christopher, and settling in Cochrane, Alberta.

That day in December, Peter had a proposition. He wanted the three Parnell brothers to do a "triathlon" – as defined by Peter – in 2003. This was not to be the traditional event we all know (i.e., swim, bike, run). No, Peter's triathlon would begin with the Calgary Marathon, followed by a tennis match and finally a round of golf. I was happy with the last two events, but the thought of running a marathon really had me worried. The last time I'd run any significant number of kilometres was in Yellowknife, for the 10 km Terry Fox Run, but that was in 1982.

What could I do? I wasn't going to lose face, especially in front of my younger brothers, so I told Pete to "bring it on." As brothers we were very competitive, so my answer was an automatic yes. This was to be the first of many physical challenges I'd set for myself in the years to come.

My first run was 1 km from my house and 1 km home along a quiet country lane. Nobody was around as I plodded up and down the snowy street, looking very much like a winterized Cliff Young, but without the stamina. It didn't take long for me to realize I had to step it up a bit, so in January 2003 I joined the Sudbury Rocks Running Club. There I met Stephanie and Vince, two of the members who put me through my paces and taught me a thing or two about running.

When I first arrived at the running club, Sudbury was experiencing a cold snap that would have been more typical for northern Ontario. Vince remembers me coming out to one of the club runs dressed like an Antarctic explorer: leather mitts with woollen inserts, a double-insulated parka with the hood up, two toques beneath the parka hood. I also had a running belt with a water bottle attachment. I guess I wasn't thinking the water bottle thing through: if it was cold enough for me to wear all that gear, it was certainly cold enough for my water supply to freeze, especially since I was wearing the running belt outside my parka. I learned pretty quickly that the water bottle strategy needed some work, as did my running gear.

Vince was the president of the club and ended up being my mentor. He helped me with shoes and gear selection, and he introduced me to the different nutrition options one must consider when contemplating a marathon.

Vince taught me that the successful road to long-distance running is a long, slow process involving minor increases in distance and speed over the course of a long training period. He said aspiring runners should take numerous breaks in their progress, to give both body and mind a rest. Of course, I did push the envelope a

NUTRITION AND GEAR: EARLY DAYS

When I started running, Vince gave me advice about the nutrition I would need for a long race. He suggested Gatorade and Clif Shots, which are energy gels containing electrolytes, sodium, potassium and magnesium. Even at the beginning of my running career, I never had problems with food or drink during or before races. I'm grateful for that! Many runners have trouble keeping food and drink down, which is literally a drag.

Because I started running in December, I learned how to run in winter conditions first – not a bad idea if you live in Canada! Some of the most important cold-weather running lessons Vince taught me along the way were:

1. There is nothing wrong with carrying water when you train in the winter. A bottle of water won't freeze as quickly if you add a bit of sugar or salt, and then place it under one layer of clothing before heading out. Alternatively, pack Gatorade or Powerade, which already include sugar and salt.
2. Even better than carrying liquid: run light. Find refreshment somewhere along the course instead.
3. Warm up energy gels in your hand (even a gloved one) for about 10 minutes before you ingest them.
4. Dress in light layers instead of going for an Ernest Shackleton look. Layers are more comfortable than a parka, and they also give you the freedom of movement you need to run faster.

Thanks, Vince!

little bit! If the experienced group was going for a two-hour training session, I sometimes went along with them.

Each Saturday morning, Stephanie, Vince and I would leave the Cambrian Fitness Centre and head off toward Lake Ramsey in the centre of the city. Soon I was running 5 and 10 km loops. To my surprise, I found I could keep up with the others, and within three months I had lost 4.5 kg. I also found that my mind had cleared – I felt better physically, but also emotionally and mentally. Running gave me a sense of purpose and clarity. It was unlike anything I had experienced, especially given the low point I had reached after losing Wendy.

Throughout this process, Vince introduced me to four different types of running sessions:

1. Hills: run up a hill and walk down ten times
2. Intervals: run 1 km and walk 0.5 km ten times
3. Tempos: run 10 km at race pace
4. Long slow runs.

We completed one of the long slow runs every Saturday; my first one was 10 km. I added distance as I progressed, increasing the length of these runs up to 20 km by May. I also ran two other times per week, taking hills, intervals and tempos in turns.

My first official race was the 5 km Sun Run, which took place in April, starting and ending at Cambrian College in Sudbury. It was a cool day and I started off fast. After 4 km I was done, and I paid the price on the last kilometre. However, I came in at 21 minutes, 5 seconds and was well pleased with the result.

By May, Vince felt I was ready for my first half-marathon. I drove to Ottawa and completed the flat fast course in 1 hour 38 minutes 10 seconds (1:38:10). I felt good, and upon returning to Sudbury I chatted to Vince about my next race. We decided I should do one more half before the Calgary Marathon in July. North Bay, only a couple of hours east of Sudbury, was running a half-marathon in early June, and that fit my schedule just fine. My training was going well: by that point I was running 25 to 30 km every Saturday. The North Bay Half-marathon was a fairly small race with around 50 runners. I pushed the pace at the start and held it until 2 km from the finish. I wanted to beat my Ottawa time and was thrilled to come in at 1:37:17.

After North Bay, I started to "taper," or back off on the volume of training. Vince told me that this was critical because it prevents overtraining before a big race and ensures the body is strong and rested. On the Saturday before I headed to Alberta to meet Peter and Andy, Vince said I was ready.

And so, in late June, feeling somewhat prepared, I flew west to Cochrane and Andy came in from his home in Cornwall, England. The "Three Devon Musketeers" gathered to set up the ground rules – negotiations ensued well into the night. Handicaps were established and venues confirmed.

Andy was the runner among us and the youngest. He was quite confident as we approached the start line of the Calgary Marathon. Of course, his home in England is at sea level, and in Calgary he would be running at an altitude of 1049 m. I wondered if the altitude difference would affect his performance enough to allow Peter and me to represent any kind of competition.

The morning of the marathon dawned hot, the sun angling down on us through that clear-blue southern-Alberta sky. When the starter's pistol went off, I flew out of the gate and felt good for the first few kilometres. Then, disaster struck. My foot went into a pothole, and my knees smashed onto the pavement. Blood poured down my legs as I struggled to stand. Although I was dazed, I kept going and crossed the finish line in second place, in 3:50:22. Not bad, but not good enough. Despite the altitude, Andy had hammered it home in 3:30:00 for a win, with Peter coming in a respectable third.

The next event was the tennis. I was the favourite and, despite stiff competition, came out on top. The following day was the final event.

THE CALGARY MARATHON

In 2010 the Scotiabank Calgary Marathon was voted the best road race in Alberta. It is also Canada's longest-running marathon, having begun on August 10, 1963, when 19 runners started out from Glenmore Stadium. Calgary's was the first official marathon to be staged in western Canada and was the brainchild of Olympic runner and Calgarian Doug Kyle. At the end of his running career, Doug was determined to bring the 1964 Olympic time trials to Calgary, where the city's high altitude and a hometown advantage would give Calgarian runners an extra edge. Combining forces with another Calgarian, Bill Wyllie, who measured the course with his car's odometer and helped Doug "beat the bushes" to come up with the 19 entrants, Doug not only won the first Calgary Marathon but also was successful in bringing the time trials to Calgary in 1964, at the second Calgary Marathon.

With his low handicap, Peter was expected to win the golf event on the Kananaskis Country course. Despite good games by Andy and me, he kept his cool and took us both at the last hole. Going over the results that night, we established that overall first place went to Peter, second to me and third to Andy. We planned a rematch for 2013 – I think I might be a contender in the marathon event this time!

It was wonderful being out west with my brothers and completing the marathon. I felt a sense of connection that I had been lacking since Wendy passed away. When I arrived back in Sudbury, I walked into my empty house, surveyed my surroundings and realized I had become stuck in a rut. Despite still living in the area, Kyle and Kristina had both left home and were settled with their respective partners. Each night I returned to an empty house. I was very grateful to have my running, which helped me to keep moving and alleviate my feeling of restlessness. I decided to begin seriously training again and set myself a goal. I signed up for the Toronto Waterfront Half-marathon and then the Toronto International Marathon. I aimed to qualify for the most prestigious marathon of them all: I wanted to run Boston.

In early September I set off for my first Toronto race, which turned out to be quite an event! The weather was perfect for the run along the stunning course around Lake Ontario, and I came in at 1:30:01. I was happy with my time, but not as pleased as two other participants were with theirs. Two world records were broken that day.

After I'd recovered, I set off for the finish line to watch the final runners coming in. I heard a lot of people talking about some guy named Ed Whitlock. I was curious. Just under three hours into the marathon, someone close to me yelled, "Ed's coming!" The crowd around me near finish line was going nuts. Ed came in at 2:59:08. This is a good marathon time but not outstanding, unless you are Ed. When he made this time that day in 2003, he was 72 years old. Ed was the first guy over 70 to have run a marathon in less than three hours. This is someone who had run as a teenager but didn't really run seriously until he was in his forties.

I felt privileged to be there to see Ed finish the race. Even though he was mobbed, I did manage to congratulate him. And there was more fun yet to come.

For the next 2½ hours I drank chocolate milk and chatted with other runners who were lingering at the finish line. Incredibly, another name was on everyone's lips: Fauja Singh. Was another world record possible? And, more to the point, how could a six-hour marathon be a record?

At just past five hours, the crowd started to go crazy again. Then we saw him. Around the final bend, surrounded by a small group of runners to guide him over the finish line, came 92-year-old Fauja.

THE TORONTO WATERFRONT MARATHON

The Toronto Waterfront Marathon began in 1990 and takes a course that begins on University Avenue and finishes downtown at City Hall, following the lakeshore. I was really impressed with the festive atmosphere at this marathon: bands played, cheerleaders cheered and there were lots of aid stations along the way. First-time marathoners love this race because of the flat fast track and the six hour cut-off time.

He crossed the line in 5:40:04, another world record, this time for 90-plus runners. Fauja had taken up running in India when he was 63, after the death of his wife and son, and got serious about the sport when he moved to the UK at the age of 81. In 2004 the *Indian Express* quoted Fauja as saying, "I run while talking to God." The man must have some inspiration and drive; at the time of this writing, he continues to compete in marathons as a centenarian. A vegetarian centenarian, actually.

Cliff Young, Ed Whitlock and Fauja Singh made me realize that it is never too late to begin running.

When I arrived back in Sudbury, I was inspired by what I'd experienced in Toronto, totally pumped to make final preparations for the Toronto International Marathon in October. I continued with my training regimen of hill repeats, tempo runs, intervals and, the key element, long slow runs. One of my fellow runners, Stephanie, had agreed to be my pacer during the race and, when the day arrived, I was ready.

Waiting at the start line, I went over my race plan. I needed to do half in 1:40:00. I was amazed when we reached the halfway point at 1:38:24! I was feeling good and aimed to maintain a pace of 4:45 per km. With a final push, I came in at 3:22:37. Running the last few hundred metres, knowing I'd qualified for the Boston Marathon was the best feeling I'd had in a long time.

After the exhilaration of the qualifying, I returned to a silent house. I also returned to work, where I was dealing with HR issues – people complaining about other people – and union negotiations. I wasn't enjoying any of it, and the prospect of working another 12 years until retirement prompted me to make a life-changing decision. I didn't realize it at the time, but the highs of running had somehow exposed me to the reality of my everyday life as something I wasn't enjoying, something I needed to change in order to find out more about myself.

Since our triathlon, I had become closer to my brother Peter. I decided I needed to strike out in a new direction, and Peter was supportive, even offering to put me up in his home in Cochrane until I'd decided what to do. One evening, I asked Kristina and Kyle to come over and explained that I wanted to resign from my job, sell the house and go and stay with Peter. They were both very supportive and understood my reasons. I was very emotional, and I felt that I was somehow abandoning them, but both kids said, "Go for it, Dad." They wanted me to be happy.

While I dismantled the life that I had built in Sudbury, I planned a trip to the UK to visit my other siblings. I was feeling freer than I'd felt in a long time. I felt that the world was suddenly opening itself up to me, and perhaps it was this sense of liberty that made me hearken back to an article I'd read a couple of months earlier in the *Toronto Star*, "Fastest Crossing of Africa, by Bike." In 2003 a group of cyclists had ridden from Cairo to Cape Town on a journey lasting four months. It was the first Tour d'Afrique. In the flush of excitement brought about by my new lease on life, I sent off my deposit and signed up for the 2005 tour. It was something to look forward to.

Sue was my support crew for the start of the Rock and Ice Ultra, a role she would play for all 250 marathons in 2010.

3
RUNNING WEST: FROM MARATHONS TO TRIATHLONS

"Our greatest glory is not in never failing,
but in rising every time we fall."

—CONFUCIUS

Who knew that a 1 km out and back jog would be a life-changing event? After Peter's "triathlon" and my decision to shake things up a bit, here I was, heading west. My interest in running continued to drive me, and I progressed from marathons to triathlons, even though that meant I had to somehow increase my ability in the swimming pool!

Things moved quickly after I'd made my decision to uproot from Sudbury. I sold the house, quit my job and headed to England to visit family. I continued to train there, running on the seashore near where my sister Jan lived, in Bournemouth on the south coast. I stayed in England through Christmas and New Year. At a party, I met a teacher named Sue. I'd been on my own for over two years and had only been out on one date, which didn't go particularly well. With Sue, I felt completely at ease. We had some great conversations in the days that followed, went out for dinner and took some beautiful walks along the beach. I even joined Sue, Jan, her husband, Austin, and Jan's friend Julie in a crazy race called the GRIM that was taking place in Aldershot. It wasn't very good training for Boston, but it was loads of fun.

The GRIM is a 12 km footrace held annually on an army vehicle testing course. The race starts with a long hill that winds down to a water-filled ravine. We dodged (or charged right through) puddles, crawled under some camouflage netting and negotiated some weird man-made mounds and more water. Basically, the GRIM is a race through large puddles and mud. We came out of it looking like a bunch of mud-spattered kids.

Eventually, however, I had to return to Canada to finish what I'd begun. I had to pack up my house and make my move west.

In February, after I'd settled myself with Peter and family in Cochrane, I finally had some joy enter my life when my Kristina gave birth to a beautiful baby girl and I became the proud "papa" to little Autumn Marie. Sue and I kept in touch, and that April I invited her to come and visit me in Canada.

I wanted her to enjoy the Rockies and booked a log cabin near Canmore. I sent her a photo and she showed it to her son, Calum. He was somewhat concerned: "Mum, you're going to stay in a garden shed in the woods with a man you hardly know!" Fortunately, Sue was able to allay his fears. After a wonderful 10 days together, Sue had to head home and back to work. I too had an engagement. At the Calgary airport, I left Sue at the check-in and headed off to catch my flight to Boston and the long-anticipated Boston Marathon.

When I first arrived in Cochrane, I had joined the local running club, which met at a café called Guy's every Saturday at 8:30 a.m. The club was run by Annie, a wonderful and welcoming redhead of Irish descent. We would all set out at the same time, and then groups would split off to run whatever distance they were inclined to cover that day. Some members of the club were just out to do a few kilometres as part of their fitness regime. Others were preparing for 10 km races and half-marathons; still others, like me, were training for a marathon. After training, everyone would congregate back at Guy's for a leisurely breakfast and to catch up with everyone's news. I'm pleased to say that the Cochrane Red Rock Running & Tri Club operates in same manner today. By joining the club, I was able to keep up my training for the Boston race.

Everything I had read about the Boston Marathon was true. I met up with friends from Sudbury's running club – Vince, Stephanie, Monique, John, Karen, Ann – as well as with a Yellowknife runner named Audrey. Early on the morning of the race, runners were bussed out to the town of Hopkinton, where we hung around in a muddy field for about three hours, until noon. Then it began. Before I started running the race, I had decided not to stress about it but rather take it as it came and enjoy the atmosphere.

With regard to the number of participants, Boston is a huge race. After the starter's pistol went off, it took Monique, Karen, Audrey and me fifteen minutes to reach the start line. They say there are over a million spectators along the route, and I can believe it! Around every bend and along every straight, crowds of people congregate to yell and cheer. I could hear the girls from Wellesley College well before they came into view.

It was an incredibly hot day, but Karen was a true pro at zigzagging through the crowds to gather up refreshments, from popsicles, Mr. Freezes, ice and jelly beans to Fig Newtons and pretzels. Even Heartbreak Hill wasn't as daunting as I'd expected. I agree with Monique, who remembers that we spent more energy weaving through the walkers than we did running.

The four of us stuck together until the 35 km mark, when Karen and Monique bolted. Audrey and I passed loads of people walking the last few kilometres, and there were quite a number laid out on the side of the road. We crossed the finish line together – my legs still feeling good – and the cheers of the crowd were fantastic. We all got together after the race, tired, caked with salt, but happy. A few post-race beers at Cheers – where I hoped someone would know my name – were a well-deserved treat.

After the race, I returned to my new life in Cochrane. At this point, I was still renting a room at Peter and Helen's, and my possessions from Sudbury were in storage. I didn't yet see the point in finding a place of my own. That summer I was planning to visit Sue in the UK and then take a trip to visit family in Australia.

When my sister Jan found out I was going to be in the UK in the summer, she mentioned that she and my two other sisters were planning to do the London Triathlon. I would be there at the right moment to participate. She asked if I would be interested in doing it with them, and I thought, "Why not?"

Of course, this would be a traditional triathlon, unlike the one I had done with my brothers the year before. I knew the run wouldn't be a problem: I had my training sewn up for the spring, and I'd already registered for a few races, including the Footstock Half-marathon in Cochrane and the Calgary Marathon. Also, I'd ridden a bike for years and felt comfortable with the idea of a long bike race. But the swim, well, that was another matter. I had no idea what kind of training I would need to engage in, or even what the race might entail, but John and Jamie, a couple of the triathletes in the Red Rock Running Club helped me out. They suggested I visit the pool in town and chat with Suzanne.

I headed to the Big Hill Leisure Pool in Cochrane, where I met Suzanne, the pool coordinator and a very experienced instructor. She saw me take to the water and just shook her head. I was pathetic. I managed to swim two lengths, but I had to keep stopping for breath. It looked like my triathlon career might be over even before it had begun. I knew it was going to be a long haul, but I was determined to persevere. Suzanne was tough but fair. She put me into the club training session and gave me a lane all to myself. The first exercise was holding a flutterboard and kicking. I went backward. She introduced me to several swimming techniques, and slowly I improved. The weeks were ticking away, and I had to be able to swim 1.5 km of the River Thames and then have enough left in me for a 40 km bike ride followed by a 10 km run around Canary Wharf.

I decided to set myself an interim goal and signed up for a May event in Calgary. It was cleverly named "Try This Triathlon." The swim, bike and run distances were shorter than the London event's, but it would be a good test for me. By this point I had spent quite a few hours in the pool, and I was relieved to find I could at least swim the number of laps required. I wasn't fast but I could cover the distance. The number-one piece of equipment that would prove invaluable relative to the swim was my wetsuit. A couple of weeks earlier I had visited Mark at Way Past Fast, a triathlon shop in Calgary. He sold the thickest wetsuit you can get, and during a test swim I realized that, with the wetsuit on, I could achieve the most important thing in swimming – I could float!

After completing the Calgary tri, I knew I could be last out of the water, overtake a few people during the bike race and then hammer the run. This would remain my game plan for all but one of my future triathlon events.

With Calgary's triathlon under my belt, I decided to do two more, the first at Arbour Lake, a small community just outside of Calgary. This was an Olympic-distance event: 1500 m swim, 40 km bike and 10 km run. The water in the lake was freezing. Thank heavens for wetsuits; mine not only gave me more buoyancy but also kept me warm. A definite lifesaver. The last race I undertook before heading to England was even more of a challenge, but it ended with a pleasant twist that would serve to enhance my triathlon "career" in ways I wasn't yet prepared to think about.

The Great White North Triathlon is popular with Cochrane triathletes. The race is a half-Ironman – a huge step up for me – which consists of a 2 km swim, 90 km bike and half-marathon run. I knew the race would really put me to the test.

On the Friday before the race, a group of us headed north on Highway 22 to Stony Plain to camp near Allan Beach on Hubbles Lake, where the swim took place. I set up my tent amid a sea of motor homes, taking comfort in knowing that if the weather turned, I could always knock on someone's door!

At 8:00 on the morning of the race, I took my place on the shoreline with 600 other racers. For me, the toughest part of any triathlon is the start. When that pistol goes off, everyone forges into the water at once. I can only compare the mayhem to a maniacal boxing match. Arms and legs are flying, and if you're in the way, too bad. I decided to hold back for a couple of minutes until the craziest part of the entry was over.

When the water wasn't quite as white as it was at the beginning, I waded out into the lake and, after two 1 km loops of the lake, I moved into transition and the bike event. I must say that this is the second toughest part of a triathlon for me. Unless the water's really warm, you have to wear a wetsuit, and because I'm not the most flexible person in the world, getting out of one is no easy task and usually adds minutes to my time. Fortunately, at the Great White North (as well as at many other triathlons), there is a wonderful band of "strippers": a team of men and women who tell you to sit and then proceed to strip you of your wetsuit. Brilliant!

The race went well and I finished in five and a half hours. While I was cooling down, someone mentioned that the Great White North was a qualifier for the International Triathlon Union (ITU) Age Group World Championships, and that I should check to see if I'd qualified in my age group. I couldn't believe I might have qualified to compete, as it would turn out, in Denmark.

I checked to see if I'd made the short list and found that I had a 50/50 chance of getting a place in the roll down. I hoped that some of the people who had qualified before me wouldn't take their places and thus give me a shot at the big time! I was eighth on the list and, fortunately, enough people gave up their spots that I was invited to join Triathlon Canada's team in my age group and compete in Fredericia, Denmark, in August 2005.

I was ecstatic. I saw the next few months' events stretching before me. Somehow I had traded my life in Sudbury, which had become so empty, for this exciting life of racing, of testing myself. This was a new feeling for me and sometimes it didn't seem real. I was pushing my limits, and sometimes it felt that I had never done anything else but train, race and enjoy the feeling that comes with the focus and drive needed for both.

THE INTERNATIONAL TRIATHLON UNION

The ITU was founded in 1989 and has its headquarters in Vancouver. It was at this meeting that 30 national federations set the Olympic distance for triathlon: 1.5 km swim, 40 km bike and 10 km run. These distances were upheld at the ITU's first world championship, held in Avignon, France, that year, with over 800 participants from 40 countries. The ITU's Dextro Energy Triathlon ITU World Championships Series became the organization's top-tier race series in 2009, with eight races in eight different countries. There are 120 national triathlon federations affiliated with the ITU.

The ITU race wasn't until the next year, 2005, after the London Triathlon, after the Tour d'Afrique. I put Fredericia on the back burner and forced myself to focus instead on the London race I was entering with my sisters. I trained hard for another month before setting off for the small village of Mudeford, on Britain's Dorset coast, where I continued to train and enjoyed a fantastic visit with Sue.

When the day of the London Triathlon arrived, Sue and I headed up to the city to meet up with my three sisters. Sally was the favourite for the bike event. She was a police officer, and her job entailed patrolling the streets of London on a mountain bike. Jan and Louise were the strong swimmers, and Louise had previously run the London Marathon. I briefly wondered how I would do, but I was also looking at the race in much the same way I had viewed the Boston Marathon: I was there to have fun.

The London Michelob Triathlon was a huge event. Some 9,000 participants competed over the course of two days. The Saturday afternoon of the race we walked our bikes along the bank of the Thames toward the site for the bike transition, commenting on the number of security officers the triathlon had employed. Seeing 9,000 bikes in one place was pretty amazing. No wonder security was tight; the total value of those bicycles must have been in the millions.

Unfortunately, we had an unpleasant experience at the beginning of the race when we watched some EMTs placing a guy in a wetsuit into an ambulance. He was one of the earlier competitors, a 47-year-old doctor who had to be pulled from the water and had, sadly, died of a heart attack. I later realized that it is very unusual for participants to pass away during triathlons.

With the cautionary tale of the doctor in mind, my sisters and I readied ourselves for the race. We pushed our bikes into what looked like an aircraft hangar, with bikes lined up as far as the eye could see. We were all in different heats, and our results were pretty mixed. I had a fun race. The swim was in the Thames, which I thought was a bit dodgy. I certainly didn't want to drink too much of the water, even though we had been assured that this stretch of river had been cleaned. Transitioning to the bike was different for me than it had been in previous races. I had had to leave my Giant 3 bike, equipped with tri bars, behind in Canada and instead I rode my brother-in-law Austin's Stump Jumper mountain bike. The bike worked well and the ride down to Tower Bridge and back was amazing. At the completion of the 40 km section on the bike, I dropped it off in the hangar and headed out on the 10 km run around Canary Wharf. My sisters, having raced in earlier heats, and Sue were on the course with signs saying, "Go, Martin, Go" and "Run, Twigglet."

By the time I returned to Canada, after my stint in Australia, winter was starting to take hold. It felt like I had been on the move for a long time, and I had. But I didn't have time to relax and enjoy my homecoming or spend much time reviewing my year of marathons and triathlons, because I now had to get my head around my cycling trip through Africa, which would begin in January 2005.

4

TOUR D'AFRIQUE:
AN EPIPHANY

"Africa seeps in and works her magic
on the hearts of even the most resistant."
—JAMES D. BROWN, Tour d'Afrique participant

When I first signed up for the Tour d'Afrique, I was in a headspace that required me to take action, move on, engage with the world in a way I hadn't before. Of course, I couldn't have known how much this "tour" I was about to engage in would affect my life in the years to come. I viewed it as an adventure, one that simultaneously allowed me to see an amazing part of the world and test the limits of my endurance on a bicycle! As I was cycling from Cairo to the Cape, the organization that I would come to associate with so wholeheartedly, Right To Play, was also on the continent, bringing its programs and support to children in communities from Sierra Leone in the west to Kenya in the east, the Sudan in the north to Mozambique in the south.

I had already arranged to have some of the vaccinations I needed for the Tour d'Afrique: hepatitis A and B, yellow fever, meningitis. I had also stocked up on anti-malarial medication, antibiotics and Imodium. But I still had to do the bureaucratic work and organize my visas. I naively thought things would be pretty straightforward. Eight of the 10 countries through which I would travel did not require me to obtain a visa, only that I pay about $25 at their borders. I did, however, have to obtain visas for Ethiopia and Sudan ahead of time.

I applied for the Ethiopian visa first, sending off my passport and hoping for a quick turnaround. Thankfully, it came back stamped within two weeks. Not bad. At this point, however, I realized I didn't have enough time to send my passport away again for the Sudanese stamp. I needed my documents to travel to the UK, where I would be spending Christmas and New Year's Eve with Sue. I decided I would just visit the Sudanese Embassy in London to get the visa.

In the meantime, I purchased a Gary Fisher bike frame at Cochrane Cycle, where a fellow named Preston set everything up for me: disc brakes with rear suspension, panniers, Goodyear tires. I also bought a tent from Mark at Trailblazers, along with a hockey bag that would hold all my gear.

The night before departure, I checked my list. The bike was boxed up, my medical kit, camping gear, clothing and bike spares were all packed. Now I just had to get it all to Cairo, via the UK. Getting from Calgary to Heathrow wasn't an issue. But then I had to take the bus down to the Dorset coast, where Sue's dad, Eric, was kind enough to pick me and my luggage up at the bus station.

By the time I got to Sue's place I was dead beat but determined to keep my energy up. In the midst of planning for the Tour d'Afrique, I had also planned something else: I had brought a ring with me, set with a Canadian diamond, a ring with which I was determined to propose to Sue. That first night at Sue's, I went to my backpack and took out the box containing the ring. I said, "I have something for you," and gave her the box.

At first, Sue looked bemused and I was somewhat concerned. After all, here was a guy who had no home and no job asking her to give up the life she knew and move to the other side of the world. I mumbled something about her not having to give me an answer straightaway and saw a look of realization appear on her face. She laughed and said she thought I was giving her a pair of earrings but had lost one en route! In the end, she was delighted that it was an engagement ring, and she said, "Yes."

Our short time together before the Africa trip was marred only by one thing: we had to cancel a celebratory trip to Prague – both to commemorate our engagement and my 50th birthday – because the Sudanese embassy took longer than expected in getting my passport ready for me. However, the tickets didn't go to waste. We gave them to Sue's dad and her son, Calum, who had a very enjoyable trip. Lesson learned: next time I cycle through 10 African countries, I'll make sure I plan to get the visas well ahead of time!

Soon it was January 12, time for me to grab my bike and head off again, this time for Cairo and the start of my four-month ride. Sue and I knew that keeping in touch would be a challenge, but we would do our best with intermittent phone calls and e-mails.

I arrived in Cairo at 2:00 a.m., jet lagged and slightly confused. A fellow named Harmy met me at the airport, and he ushered me, my bike box and hockey bag to the Cataract Hotel, where I tried to sleep for a few hours before breakfasting at 9:30 the next day.

While in Cairo, I met the folks who would be doing the tour with me, some of whom joined me on a variety of outings around the city. The 28 men and four women on the tour were from Holland, Canada, the UK, South Africa, Switzerland, France and Germany.

First, Randy, the tour director helped me get my bike in order. I tested my bike with South Africans Martin and Henning, who rode with me to visit the pyramids at Abu Sim. The roads we travelled on that trip were covered with sisal, and we stopped to watch men collect the grass and bail it, after which it would be made into rope. I also met Patrick from Canada and Jack, an American, who accompanied Martin and me to the Cairo Museum. Tut was there, of course, but so was an amazing animal mummification exhibit. The blue mummified hedgehog was touted as a cure for baldness in the afterlife. Sign me up!

Before heading south to Cape Town from the pyramids at Giza, we had a tour briefing. We learned how to have a shower with a cup of water and how to protect ourselves from attacking dogs, among other items. Randy also went over the racing component of the tour. Some participants were there to compete and accumulate the best times during the various races (or stages) set out along the

Above: The Tour d'Afrique riders prepare to leave Cairo from the pyramids at Giza. Below: Desert campsite in Egypt.

course as we made our way to the Cape. I was in high spirits, not able to predict what was to come in the next four months.

It would take the rest of the month of January for us to make our way south through Egypt to the Sudan. We biked 30 km through Cairo's smoggy air to the city's outskirts then embarked on the flat, sandy road littered with burned-out tires. Our days involved between 105 and 190 km of biking, substantial meals like beef stew and rice, some hazards (saddle sores, crashes and illness) and many scenes and tastes and sounds I will not forget in my lifetime: the view of the Red Sea from a little cafe as I drank a Fanta; a sweet breeze alleviating my huffing and puffing as we ascended mountainous terrain, moving inland to Qena, then Luxor; feeling small amidst the hieroglyphic-covered limestone giants at the temple of Hatshepsut; sweet, strong tea; the Nile, its green cultivated banks and the desert pushing in from all sides; five camels in the back of a pickup; a loudspeaker in Idfu blaring prayers all night, except when the "DJ" switched it up and played Aqua's "Barbie Girl" instead; and of course, the Aswan Dam and the relocated temples of Ramses II at Abu Simbel.

I sometimes rode with the lead pack, sometimes with the second group and other times bringing up the rear. At first, a Dutch rider named Aris seemed to be in the lead as he won two out of the first four stages of the race, but before we reached the Sudan, Aris fell and broke his collar bone. He was airlifted to Amsterdam and returned to us two days out of Khartoum. Egypt presented difficulties to me as well: brake trouble (which bike mechanic Ewald helped me fix), tire-pressure issues, sore knees and bum, as well as gut ache, all combined to make parts of the trip something of a test of character!

By the time we reached Aswan and headed out on a felucca on the Nile, the tour's nurse, Edi, was giving me 600 mg of Ibuprofen at a time, along with plenty of fluids and some anti-inflammatory spray for my knees. When I was feeling low, I was thankful to be able to ride slowly with Dave Williams, a fellow Canadian.

RIGHT TO PLAY IN AFRICA, 2005

As I prepared to make my way by bicycle from the pyramids, through Egypt and on south to South Africa, I didn't know about the children's charity Right To Play, but RTP had already spent over five years in many of the countries I would be cycling through. The organization began as an Olympic Committee legacy project that Norwegian Olympian speed skater Johann Olav Koss was part of. The project was based on a vision to make the world better, healthier and safer for kids living amidst poverty, violence, illness and upheaval. Up until this point, the organization, then called Olympic Aid, had brought sport and play programs to refugee communities in Africa, starting with Côte d'Ivoire and Angola in 2001. These programs promoted health education and healthy lifestyle choices. By the time I was cycling through the continent in 2005, Koss's organization had changed its name to Right To Play and was in the process of decentralizing by creating regional offices throughout the world to better serve communities. In Africa, the first to receive regional offices were Uganda and Sierra Leone.

Up until 2005, RTP had relied on eager international volunteers to implement its programs. Right To Play had learned a lot over its first five years about how sport could effect change in kids' lives, how their behaviour and ability as leaders improved as they took part in activities that allowed them to practise cooperation and leadership skills as they gained self-confidence. However, RTP also knew it needed to change its delivery model to be sustainable – the keen volunteers RTP imported to communities the world over were great, but they didn't stay in those communities, so they couldn't give the kind of ongoing support to kids that Right To Play wanted to provide. So, in 2005, RTP started hiring and training local staff and leaders to support and deliver programs. During this period, RTP switched from having 400–500 international volunteers to training 15,000 local staff and volunteers, on the ground, wherever RTP was giving support. Right To Play training allowed some volunteers to become RTP staff, coaches and leaders – and it has allowed others different opportunities within their communities.

Another change was also afoot in 2005 – RTP was branching out from refugee camps and starting to touch other communities of people with its programs, trying to reach as many kids as it could.

We also encountered our share of political upset, which made for some bumps in the tour. Our boat trip from Abu Simbel across Lake Nasser to Wadi Halfa in the Sudan, for example, became our boat trip from Aswan to Wadi Halfa: the Ministry of Defence had disallowed our original plan due to an "issue of national security." At this point I was on a diet of Ibuprofen, Imodium – diarrhea had arrived on the scene – Tylenol and CIPRO (an antibiotic), and the backtracking to Aswan was uncomfortable. The Sudan found me in better spirits, though, especially when the CIPRO kicked in.

The Sudan is a dry country with most roads composed of a washboard base covered with sand. In my first five hours I fell eight times – that evening I changed my slick tires for fat knobby ones, and I swapped my clipless pedals for flats. This seemed to help, but the back roads presented difficult terrain throughout this part of the tour.

My 3 litre CamelBak was a lifesaver in the Sudan because it allowed me to drink continuously. I always seemed to be parched! My other daily essentials, carried with me in the panniers, were a first-aid kit, Handi Wipes and toilet paper, SPF 30 sunscreen, power bars, and two extra bottles of water. Of course, none of this could help with the fatigue which sometimes caught me on the road. On the way to Dongola I had to stop and have a nap in the shade of a bush. I was awakened by a group of small children who seemed to have been wondering what they'd found. Instead of getting back on my bike, I was able to catch a lift with one of the tour trucks, christened Betsy, which was full of the walking (or biking) wounded: pulled muscles, blisters, scrapes. A rather sorry-looking bunch!

It was in the Sudan that I first really noticed the kids. As we moved in convoys through towns like Karma – 30 white people on bikes wearing garish cycling shirts and spandex, basically looking like the circus coming to town – young people would gather and watch us. It was also in the Sudan that I started to see how the kids came alive in the town squares with their soccer balls, how the soccer stadiums were often the focal points of the communities. As we pushed through the desert on the sliver of bumpy asphalt that allowed us to observe the infinity of sand without having to fight through it – stopping at desert cafes to drink Cokes and wonder at the Tatooine-like surroundings, never staying long enough to do more than briefly meet local people – I began to wonder about the children in the communities.

One fellow Henning and I met at a pop stand near Khartoum invited us to have tea with him. We discovered that he had three wives and his friend had two; between them they had 14 children. My view of the world and its children widened.

Slowly we made our way to Khartoum, with some mishaps and tragedies along the way. Hunney, from Holland, was hit by a car but was lucky: she only had to get some stitches and straighten out her back wheel. Arnold, also Dutch, fell off his bike and broke his hip as we neared the Ethiopian border. But worst of all, 61-year-old Alfons, from Switzerland, died of a heart attack after not feeling well and getting on the truck to rest. He fell asleep and didn't wake up – we were only days from the Ethiopian border at that point. I wondered how many of us would make it to Cape Town. I was finding the trip extremely challenging and just hoped I could hang in there until the end.

As we made our way through the desert past Khartoum and

toward the Ethiopian border and the mountain city of Gondar, we began to see small, scrubby bushes on the side of the road, and the sand became dry, brown soil. When we crossed into Ethiopia, we were in a landscape similar to that of Arizona, with mountains and dry, hot conditions. By 11:00 a.m. one day I had already drunk the water in the CamelBak plus the 2 litres in my panniers, and when Betsy rumbled toward me, I decided to call it a day. Some days, especially on the inclines, I only covered 45 km before I decided to abandon the bike in favour of the truck.

On the way to Gondar, I was again struck by the soccer-loving kids. Thierry Henry befriended me and told me he was an Arsenal striker. He said he and his friends all wore the soccer jerseys of their favourite teams, most of which were from the UK's premier league. Soccer was a common language; the kids knew the names of all the top players. Amongst herdsmen on their donkeys, in between the goats and chickens in the villages, all the soccer talk seemed surreal, but Thierry's face lit up at the opportunity to talk to me about the sport.

Late one morning, I was riding through a small village in Ethiopia. The sun was high in the sky and I was covered in dust. I noticed two young boys playing table tennis at the side of the road. It brought back memories of my teens and playing at the Catholic Youth Club in Devon. I couldn't resist.

Jumping off my bike, without saying a word, I indicated that I would like to play. One of them gave me his bat and within five minutes, 100 kids had gathered around the table yelling and shouting. They seemed to come from nowhere. I must have looked strange, a tall, skinny white guy in spandex shorts and a maple leaf shirt, helmet and bike shoes. I played for about 20 minutes. I lost to both his superior technique and enthusiasm. I'm convinced I must have been up against the Ethiopian U13 champion.

At the time, I wondered why that ping-pong table was sitting there by the side of the road. Looking back, I regard this simple event as an epiphany. It made me realize the power of sport and play and how it brings people together, regardless of age, culture, language or religion.

Besides soccer games and ping-pong tables, other developed-world influences in Ethiopia included disappointing Internet cafes, a network of trenches destined to help establish telecommunications in the country, and a beautiful paved road that began about 30 km outside of dusty Gondar and stretched toward Bahar Dar. A Chinese contractor was laying the new road, planning to create a thoroughfare that would stretch from north to south in Ethiopia. Of course, the country's religious leanings also trickled in from Western culture, if centuries ago. We were privileged to visit two Orthodox monasteries on islands in Lake Tana one day, and saw Christian artifacts dating back to the 14th century.

By the time we reached the monasteries, we were a third of the way through the tour and had travelled over 3000 km. I was in 29th place, 51 hours behind the lead cyclist, Kim from Denmark. Some days I hitched a ride on Betsy or Sweetness, another of the tour's trucks, others I cycled – it depended on the day, the weather and how I was feeling. Before reaching the border with Kenya, we had many more kilometres to travel on the amazing paved road. We traversed the Blue Nile Gorge: a drop of 1300 m into 49°c temperatures, followed by an ascent of 18 km. (I hitched a ride up after almost evaporating at the bottom of the gorge!) We learned where Bob Marley's wife lived – next door to one of our campsites near Addis Ababa – and met other Rastafarians near Shashemene, including a Swedish juice-bar owner named Sven.

Kids continued to lined the roads, watching us cycle past. Sometimes I just yelled out "Kenya! Martin! 50! Canada!" which seemed to answer most of their questions. Soon, however, the roadside fans were gone, and we crossed the border into Kenya, swapping greetings of *Salaam* for *Jambo*, birr for shillings and St. George beer for Tusker lager.

My first few days in Kenya were tough because I was feeling

Above: Two Maasai boys barter water for a photo.
Below: Mr. and Mrs. Zulu's son and daughters.

rough. The road was bad all the way through the lava fields of northern Kenya, a barren place broken up only by the odd volcanic boulder. The washboard, rutted and gullied road presented problems for all the riders, even Kim and Martin, the tour's leaders. The

YONAS TADESSE:
RIGHT TO PLAY COACH AND COACH TRAINER

Yonas was born in Kirkos, near Addis Ababa, and is a polio survivor who was permanently disabled by the disease. He had attended school as a young boy but discontinued his education in Grade 10 when he could no longer bear the discrimination he faced every day. Because he was treated poorly by others, he shied away from people and activities that involved others: "I was always worried and frightened when physical and sport education class came up ... I was very much discouraged and alienated."

In May 2005, not long after I cycled through Addis Ababa, Yonas was selected to be trained as a Right To Play volunteer coach. He couldn't believe the chance he had been given. He had trouble thinking he was worth recruiting, but he convinced himself to take the training, which helped him develop a sense of self-confidence, enthusiasm and motivation. When he graduated from the training, he began inviting children and youth to join a team he was forming. Slowly but surely he became a popular Right To Play coach in his community, gaining the respect of elders and leaders, who began bringing children to his programs. Yonas also began receiving invitations to speak about discrimination and exclusion.

Today, Yonas runs RTP programs three times a week for more than 45 children with disabilities, and as a coach trainer he leads training sessions for potential coaches.

race to Marsabit presented one of the toughest riding days yet, but we were rewarded with the opportunity to watch an Arsenal vs. Bolton game in the FA Cup quarter finals in the informal setting of Jey Jey's shed – literally, a shed – a local Arsenal stronghold.

After Arsenal won the game, I met a fellow named Paul who was working with 10 HIV-infected orphans in Marsabit. I was touched by his work and we chatted for a long time before I gave him a donation and my e-mail address.

Elephants stomped through one of our campsites, the roads alternated between heavenly and horrible, and ants and bees plagued us off and on. By the halfway point in the tour, Mount Kenya was sighted in the distance and we set up camp at Isiolo, in the middle of a rolling countryside that reminded me of Devonshire. The real push was on for the capital, Nairobi, where we were able to shop in a supermarket and experience real high-speed Internet without power outages, the last high-speed connection before Cape Town. It was good to get in touch with Sue.

Periodically throughout the tour I chose to stay in a hotel instead of the designated campsites. It was good to get clean every once in a while and sleep on a real bed instead of my Thermarest, which had sprung a leak by this time. In Nairobi, I spent my day and evening off at a hotel before we headed out of town in a convoy, racing some nasty rain clouds that caught up to us just after lunch, belting us with huge warm droplets and causing torrents of water to run down both sides of the road and sometimes across it. It was soggy enough to warrant my decision to take a hotel room again at that evening's campsite – two nights in a row, luxury!

The rains of Africa, indeed. Mud and rain would be the theme for the first part of our Tanzanian travels. Rain fell, soaking the lions and hippos and elephants as some of us took a couple of days to explore the Ngorongoro Crater. It fell some more during the night, seeping into our tents and our sleeping bags. The heavens opened as we travelled down mud roads and paved roads, washboard paths and sandy stretches. I fell in the rain a couple of times. And it rained as I patched my back tire tube over and over again. After the capital city of Dodoma, I realized there were a few thorns in the tire that had been puncturing the tubes. Eventually, near the town of Mbeya, Randy lent me a big, fat, slick tire that made my bike look like a chopper!

All of my flat tires gave me pause along the road, however, time to meet a few people, from the Maasai Isaac who helped me change my first flat to the two young men who brought me back to their house after I'd broken my pump. I drank many cups of chai along the route, which helped warm the belly, especially at Geremah's mud hut on a day when the sun actually peeked through the clouds. I admired fields of sunflowers, which stood out against the dark rain clouds. And one day, before the purple-bellied clouds poured down on us again, and while the truck driver filled up with diesel, I passed some time near a dry riverbed and photographed numerous jewel-coloured butterflies.

Back in Ethiopia, when I felt I was riding Betsy too often, I had made a deal with myself that I would try to bicycle at least 10,000 km of the trip, or 87 per cent of the total distance. At Day 80, as we passed into the lake-centred nation of Malawi, I had ridden 60.3 per cent of my target distance, had my bum in the saddle for 307 hours and 15 minutes at an average speed of 19.6 km/h. By this point, I was saying that I had a United Nations bike, with various parts donated from different members of the tour: front inner tube, André (Holland); front tire and rear inner tube, Pat (Canada); rear tire, tour leader Randy (Canada); handle bar extensions, Ewald (Holland); pump, Earl (U.S.); seat post clamp, Dr. Bonnet (France); front wheel pin, Martin (South Africa); and the rest, Preston (Cochrane, Canada). I had had 25 flat tires and my body had been similarly punctured by various falls and illnesses and two big crashes.

Needless to say, I was looking forward to a day at the Chitimba Beach Resort on Lake Malawi, and a rest day. The lake is 600 km long and 100 km at its widest point. We were afforded an amazing view of it on our next biking day, after ascending 1000 m in 12 km. The climb was killer, but the rest of the day was amazing. We travelled along a ridge road, stopped for refreshments and listened to a children's choir ring out from a hall across the road from the pop stand. Malawi is a combination of water, lush vegetation and pine forest. Over the course of the trip, we rode past several timber mills and watched local people carrying several lengths of finished lumber on their heads.

At Lilongwe, the nation's capital, Arnold rejoined our group. He was the guy who broke his hip way back in Ethiopia and flew back to Amsterdam for surgery. He showed us the x-ray: two pins! I wondered: during what other race could one break a hip, fly out for surgery, come back and still be in contention for a stage win? His return encouraged me to get some serious kilometres in before the tour was over.

When we passed into Zambia, I decided to take part in some stages. First, an Ironman-distance day – I rode along a path fringed by tall grass, flowers and men chopping down undergrowth with machetes. I complete 193 km in 9.5 hours. Not bad. A few days later, I did a half-Ironman: 90 km nonstop. With long descents and short climbs, I made the distance in 3.5 hours, pulling in to the Chainama Resort in Lusaka, Zambia's capital, at 9:48 a.m.

Of course, Zambia wasn't all about the cycling. The people were friendly, especially the children. One boy I met in Mazabuka, 11-year-old Laslo Badd, was an amazing banjo player. His instrument was homemade, all wood, including the tuning pins. And it was in Zambia, near one of our bush camps, that once again I was treated to a view of another way of life, another definition of family and community.

After setting up our tents at one end of a field, Ed, André and I decided to visit what seemed to be a small village about 500 m away. When we walked over, we met Mr. and Mrs. Zulu, who offered us fresh peanuts and invited us to visit their farm. What at first appeared to be a village was actually Mr. Zulu's farm and the houses he built for himself, his three wives and his children – six boys and seven girls. The farm seemed productive, with crops of maize, tobacco and peanuts, as well as livestock: cattle, turkeys and chickens. The main farmhouse was equipped with a television, couches draped with embroidery and a wall of family photographs. Mr. Zulu suggested he would give Ed 100 acres if Ed married one of his daughters. Instead, Ed helped one of the daughters hook up a team of oxen, almost getting gouged in the process!

Laslo Badd, age 11, plays his home made banjo. After we all went for ice cream.

BENJAMIN NZOBONANKIRA: ASSISTANT NATIONAL TRAINING OFFICER, BURUNDI

"If it wasn't for sport, we could not have different ethnic groups in my community playing together and trying to resolve their differences. Through sport, they have become committed to working together toward the objectives of reconciliation and for the greater development of the country."

In 2010 Benjamin Nzobonankira travelled to Vancouver, Canada, and took part in a panel discussion with RTP's founder, Johann Olav Koss, Stephen Lewis and Wilfried Lemke: Sport, Peace and Development: How Can Sport Contribute to Positive Social Change? Benjamin's story is testament to how this is possible.

He was born in 1983 in the northern Burundian province of Kirundo, but was forced to run from his home when conflict broke out, first to Rwanda just before the 1994 genocide, then on to the Democratic Republic of Congo, which he also had to flee because of the Banyamulenge War in 1996. He was on the move again, this time through the forest, travelling hundreds of kilometres on foot to a refugee camp in western Tanzania, then on to another camp in northwest Tanzania, called Lukole, where he stayed for more than 12 years, in all that time never going beyond the camp's boundaries. There, he was able to complete his secondary schooling. He lost much during his flight from Burundi, including his mother and sister.

While at the camp, Benjamin became involved with Right To Play. He says that RTP arrived at a sensitive time in the camp, when youth were facing some problems. Many were being recruited to join rebel groups in Burundi, but RTP gave kids an alternative. Sport gave Benjamin relief and allowed him to relax, it allowed him and his friends to laugh again, and to live peacefully together. He credits his work with RTP, including time spent as a community volunteer at the camp, with his ability to learn tolerance and a new perspective on the circumstances in the countries he had fled, which had made him an exile and deprived him of his childhood.

When Benjamin returned to Burundi, he started working with RTP and is now the assistant national training officer. He said, "The skills and knowledge I acquired as a volunteer with Right To Play in the refugee camp are my tools which I have been using to integrate into the new community since my repatriation. These skills can be very important tools of reconciliation and sustainable peace in our country after such a long period of agony and conflict."

LIVE SAFE PLAY SAFE: RIGHT TO PLAY IN ZAMBIA

One of Right To Play's programs is called Live Safe Play Safe, which helps mobilize communities around the health issue of HIV/AIDS awareness and prevention, in a fun and social way. The year I cycled through Africa, RTP was delivering Live Safe Play Safe programs to communities in Tanzania, Uganda, Ethiopia, Sierra Leone, Benin, Ghana, Mali, Rwanda and Zambia.

By the end of 2005, 40.3 million people were living with HIV/AIDS, of which 17.5 million were women and 2.3 million were children under 15. The epidemic was rooted in gender and social inequalities throughout the world, which means that women and children were some of the hardest hit in affected communities. In so many places in the world, girls and women have low social and economic status and a lack of education, and they are economically dependent on and often victimized by men. In 2004 about 15 million kids had lost parents to the disease – and most of these kids were living in Africa.

Right To Play's Live Safe Play Safe programs (as well as its other programs) embrace inclusiveness, ensuring that women and girls learn how to protect themselves against the epidemic. Using physical activity and active discussions, RTP engages youth, encouraging them to prevent HIV/AIDS. Games such as Condom Tag (wherein one is safe from being tagged "HIV/AIDS" when he or she has a condom balloon in hand; players help those being chased by HIV/AIDS by passing them balloons) and Don't Trust Your Eyes (which engages youth in discussion about HIV/AIDS stigma and discrimination) help participants learn about taking care of themselves and one another, relative to the HIV/AIDS epidemic. As Lillian Kisolo Nabuduwa, a Right To Play coach in Sironko, Uganda, said in 2005, "Sport-based programs like ours ... are helping to save lives. When we share messages with the youth in our programs, we equip them with the knowledge. They then safeguard themselves and they don't have unprotected sex."

When we walked over to Mr. Zulu's farm the next day to say goodbye and give them a gift of power bars, he presented us each with a hand-carved wooden stool. We were all grateful for such a welcome and such kindness. Of course, not all people of Zambia lived in such secure and wealthy circumstances. Zambia, like most of the countries we had already cycled through, is a country populated mostly by those living in poverty. It is also a country currently experiencing an HIV/AIDS epidemic.

In 2012 more than 1 million Zambians had HIV/AIDS, and the number of those affected was almost 1 million when I was there in 2005. What I didn't know at the time was that as a result of this epidemic, 85,000 children were then living with HIV/AIDS and 630,000 had been orphaned because of the disease. Statistics were similar, in some cases more pronounced, in all the other countries we'd cycled through, except for Sudan, Ethiopia and Egypt.

The day we passed into Botswana, I completed a time trial: 65 km in 2:21:00; Kim won the race in 1:52:00. I remember Botswana for the long flat rides and the wildlife. Our boat safari through Chobe National Park was both peaceful and exhilarating: hippos, elephants, kudus, a baby crocodile and many different birds. And, on the day I made it to 7746 km on the bike (the distance from Vancouver to Signal Hill in St. John's, Newfoundland), a few of us found ourselves on our own personal "bicycling" safari when we rode slowly past a bull elephant washing himself in a water hole near the road.

Botswana seemed to fly by, and I didn't meet many people on the road or anywhere else. Donkeys, cows and horses, wildlife at Chobe, along the road and in the Okavango Delta, but people were few and far between. I still wonder why! I found myself missing Sue, my daughter Kris, granddaughter Autumn and my son Kyle all the more as I rode the deserted, flat roads, up to 200 km per day. Soon, we crossed into Namibia – a land of desert, few animals and even fewer people, it seemed, than in Botswana.

May in Namibia was dry but cold; I wore my jacket inside my

An elephant taking an early morning bath in the Chobe National Park.

sleeping bag to stay warm at night. Our route skirted the north-ern edge of the Kalahari Desert and rolled onward to Windhoek ("windy corner" – the country's capital), where William, André and I were kicked out of the Windhoek Golf & Country Club for not wearing the appropriate attire. The shame of it all passed quickly and was replaced with elation when I passed the 9000 km mark as we cycled away from Windhoek, nearing the Tropic of Capricorn.

The wind followed us from "windy corner": a tailwind pushed us forward even as a headwind held us back. Alan and I drafted one another for 75 km to save some energy one day when the headwind was particularly strong.

Namibia is a landscape that welcomes the desperate and the strong-willed: employment was at a low when I was there, and this was evident in the town of Tses, where tin and wood shacks were encircled by barbed-wire fencing and the shop counters encased in mesh and bars. But we also felt the presence of those who come to Namibia for Namibia's sake: at Garies Park, where we camped one night, we met the life-sized puppets created by an eccentric artist who made his home there. I could see why some would choose to live in this awe-inspiring environment. Through the sand and sparse vegetation of the Namib Desert we found amazing sunsets, a particularly welcome hot springs at Ai Ais in the Namibian mountains, and of course the gateway to the last country on our tour: South Africa.

As I approached the end of the tour, I became less and less motivated to ride and more inclined to take the truck! However, I was determined to cycle that 10,000 km, and so I strategized about when and how long I would ride each day. By Garies, I was 97 km away from my goal.

On May 12 the moisture from the previous night's rain hung in the air and I cycled through an area that reminded me of Dartmoor in Devon, particularly of a certain hike I had done there, the Ten Tors event, which left me and two hiking companions lost in the fog at one point! At 12:59 p.m. I hit the 10,000 km mark and celebrated with Ed and Giles and some strawberry power bars. I continued to cycle for another 150 km before reaching that night's rest stop.

The next few days of the tour skirted the Atlantic, which was too cold for a swim, along bumpy dirt roads that flattened our tires and our spirits. But our last day, the triumphal ride into Cape Town, was good. The wind was behind us and we rode the 70 km to the city's outskirts, then convoyed the final 20 km to Mouille Point. Hundreds were there to cheer us on.

When I was leaving South Africa, I knew that Africa would always be with me. I certainly had no immediate plans to head back, but something in me had definitely been awakened. The physical exertion of the tour had taken its toll, and I would need some time to recover. However, the real impact of the Tour d'Afrique was mental and spiritual, and the effects would take years to unfold.

As I headed home to reunite with my family and friends, I thought about all the wonderful stories I had to share, about companionship, landscapes and the faces of the hundreds of children I had seen along the way.

THE TOUR BY NUMBERS

1 Gary Fisher bike
2 big crashes
3 bruised ribs
4 months on the road
5 times I cleaned my bike
5 hours 41 minutes per day average time in the saddle
9 nationalities on the tour
10 countries visited
12 pounds lost
14 jars of Marmite consumed
16 rolls of toilet paper
20.4 km/h average speed across Africa
22 anti-malaria pills
28th in the race
33 flat tires
50°C hottest day
71.2 km/h maximum speed
94 days of porridge
334 postcards
833 photos
1589 km in Betsy
10,333 km pedalled
11,882 km ridden by members of the EFI club ... and uncountable yells, cheers and waves from the children across the continent of Africa

5

ALMOST AN IRONMAN

"Life's battles don't always go to the strongest or fastest man,
but sooner or later, the man who wins
is the fellow who thinks he can."

—STEVE PREFONTAINE

Coming down from Africa was difficult, but it was made easier by the busy work I had to do to get ready for Sue's arrival. I felt that my life was finally coming back together – and I continued to train. Slowly I started reaching beyond the scope of the marathon and the triathlon, and I began entertaining the idea of competing in an Ironman. Fortunately Sue didn't think I was crazy!

My bike flew to Calgary and I flew to Sue. It was a quick visit. She had given notice at the school where she had been teaching and was in the midst of arranging to move to Canada. This was a very challenging time for her and certainly a time of mixed emotions. I had made it clear that I had no desire to settle back in England. This meant that to be with me, Sue had to give up her 30-year career in teaching, a home by the sea and most importantly her son, Calum, who was just about to start university, as well as her parents, other family and friends.

I realized she must really love me, and I knew we were going to have a great future together. Now all I had to do was return to Cochrane and find us a home. Eventually I found the perfect place, next to the Bow River, with a red-rock path near the backyard, perfect for running. In the future both Sue and I would make good use of that pathway!

In the meantime, my next task was coming up in August: the ITU triathlon in Fredericia, Denmark, a beautiful old fortress town on the Jutland peninsula. The qualifier for this race, the Great White North Triathlon, is a half-Ironman, but Fredericia was something else: a 3 km swim, 120 km bike and 30 km run. Almost an Ironman. That spring, Cochrane had had the worst floods in a decade and the poor weather forced me to train indoors: spinning and plenty of treadmill work. Of course, I had recently had a great deal of practice on a bicycle, and as I started running again I quickly found my stride. I was still an inefficient swimmer, though. I had not improved much in the water, despite the best efforts of Suzanne at Big Hill, who'd taught me all she knew. I think the main issue was that I had no buoyancy. Again I decided I would just get through the swim as best as I could and focus on the biking and running.

I participated in a number of races in June and July, the highlight of which was an Olympic-distance triathlon in Edmonton. This was part of the World Masters Games, which is held every four years. There are over 16,000 participants and the age range is 30-plus. I completed the course in 2:48:41, my best time at this distance.

In July, after I'd moved into the new house, I was delighted to receive my Team Canada gear from Triathlon Canada: a very smart jacket, shorts and tops. I didn't meet the other team members until I was in Denmark. There were two elite athletes in the group: Jasper Blake and Julie Curwin. The rest of us were "age groupers" – amateur athletes of any age who compete within a group categorized by gender and a five-year age bracket – from around Canada.

Soon enough I was all set to head off to Denmark, where Sue would join me. Once we had arrived at the athletes' hotel, I met competitors from some of the other countries, along with all the other age groupers. These folks were like me: they had qualified in their own countries for the age-group race at Fredericia. They were a great bunch, and Sue and I felt welcome. As we chatted with the other athletes, I learned that the swim event would take place in the Baltic Sea! Not to worry, I told myself. I knew that the compulsory wetsuit would buoy me up amongst all the other thrashing

NUTRITION FOR AN IRONMAN

Between March 2004 and January 2008 I shifted gears and moved into triathlons, completing two Ironman Canada races by 2008. In doing this, I extended the average time I would be racing from 4.5 hours (marathon) to 16.5 hours (Ironman), thereby changing my nutrition needs. I had to take electrolytes every hour to keep my sodium and potassium levels up, and so I had to learn to eat and drink as I rode my bike. No hands! I would eat bananas, power bars and GU energy gels during my races, leaving behind the Clif Shots. I continued to drink Gatorade, which seemed to provide the right balance of potassium, sodium, sugars and carbohydrates.

bodies. At the time, I was oblivious to the other aquatic "obstacles" we would soon encounter.

I didn't sleep much the night before the race; 5:00 a.m. came around pretty quickly. At breakfast the air was thick with a mixture of emotion, stress, anticipation and excitement. I tried to gulp down some food, and then we headed to the start line.

The starter's pistol went off and we hit the water. It was freezing. Everyone thrashed around like a school of frenzied piranhas. It turned out we swimmers weren't the only ones laying claim to the sea near Fredericia that morning. Our vegetable opponents were various species of seaweed that ensnared our legs and bodies, making us feel straitjacketed. Even worse, however, were the animals, jellyfish that were as big as dinner plates and stung like hell.

The swim seemed to last for an eternity.

When I finally dragged myself up onto the shore, I was last out of the water, but I refused to wallow in self-pity. It was time to concentrate on transitioning. The bike section went well, three 40 km loops through the countryside and back into town. I clicked along, overtaking several other riders, and then I hit the run. I felt great and covered the distance in three hours. That evening, at supper, everyone was talking about their race. As always in races of this kind, some athletes achieved personal bests while others failed to finish. For me, Fredericia was an amazing experience. I felt proud that I had represented my adopted country and given my best.

In August Sue came to Canada, and we equipped our new home with everything IKEA. Then we settled in. Sue knew what she was getting into when she agreed to become my fiancée, so she wasn't surprised when we didn't hang around Cochrane for very long before it was time for me to compete in another race.

Ironman Canada is a tough race to get into. You or a friend have to be in Penticton the day after the race to sign up for the following year. Fortunately my friends Pam and Dan signed me up in 2004 for the 2005 event. It was now time to undertake the training for the serious distances required of its participants. Rated one of the best Ironman events on the planet, Subaru Ironman Canada entails a 3.8 km swim, a 180 km bike and a full marathon (42.2 km) run.

I had been training with the tri guys from the club and had been given lots of valuable tips. For the swim, I was told to use Glide, a lubricant, around my ankles and wrists to ease wetsuit removal, as well as around my neck to reduce wetsuit friction burns. I was also told to start off at the back of the pack so I wouldn't get beaten up in the early stages, and to look up and spot the turn buoys every 12 strokes or so. For the bike, my friends recommended that I reduce the pressure in my tires before leaving my bike in the transition area. They also suggested I slap on sunblock before heading out, and that I eat and drink a lot during the bike event; this is the time to load up prior to the run. Finally, for the run, tips included: keep taking in water, nutrition and electrolytes during the run; don't panic when the legs feel like rubber after coming off the bike; and use a run–walk system to steady the pace. My advice to all tri athletes: if you're bald like me, wear a hat!

On the Friday before the race, Sue and I drove to a campground near Lake Skaha in Penticton. I love camping in a tent, but Sue had never experienced a night under canvas, and it took her a while to get used to the idea. I surprised her with the gift of an extra thick, top-of-the-line Thermarest, not the usual half-inch model but the full, one-inch deluxe. I could tell how impressed she was by her response: she was speechless.

SUBARU IRONMAN CANADA

What would become Ironman Canada started in Penticton as an ultra distance event in 1983 with 23 participants. By 1986 the event had morphed into the North American mainland Ironman, covered by CBC and with 348 participants. That year, records were set in both men's and women's races: Dave Kirk with 0.20.21 and Tracey Bell Kelly with 11:27:33. It wasn't until 1990 that a purse prize was offered, US$50,000, and the field grew to 890 racers. Ironman Canada is organized by the World Triathlon Corporation (WTC) and is a qualifier for the Ironman World Championship held annually in Hawaii.

Sponsors for the race have included Budweiser, Timex and the current sponsor, Subaru. The event is one of the most respected Ironman races in the world and has been the site of numerous records, triumphs and heartwarming stories, including that of Louie Bonpua, who suffered from leukemia and reached his lifetime goal of completing an Ironman in 2001 at Ironman Canada before passing away in 2002.

Ironman Canada puts on a fantastic pasta dinner followed by presentations on the Saturday evening before the race. The atmosphere was incredible, with over 2,000 people packed into a giant hall. The highlight of the evening was hearing the main speaker, Sister Madonna Buder, otherwise known as The Iron Nun.

Like me, Sister Madonna began competing in races later in life, having begun training at the age of 48 in order to feed her mind, body and spirit. In 1985, at age 55, she completed her first Ironman event and to date has completed over 325 triathlons, holding age-group records in a variety of races. Sister Madonna's example would come to my mind in 2009 when I began running to raise money for Right To Play; she trains and races, but she also raises money for a variety of charities.

That night in Penticton, Sister Madonna entranced the audience with her determination and grace. She would be the first female to compete in Ironman Canada's 75–80 age group. She told us she wanted to be the first woman to compete in the 80–85 age group in 2010 (which she did). After her inspirational talk, we all headed back to the campground, deep in our own thoughts, with just enough time to make final preparations for the following day and try to get some sleep.

The next morning dawned clear and hot; I knew it was going to be a gruelling day. The day before, Sue and I had deposited my bike at the first transition. One of the old timers there repeated the tip my tri buddies had already imparted: let some air out of the bike tires because the air in the tubes has been known to expand in the heat of the day prior to the race and cause tires to explode. Good grief. Arriving on the bike transition, I pumped my tires up, then Sue and I made our way down to Okanagan Lake's shoreline where the race's participants had already gathered. All competitors were dressed in black neoprene wetsuits and everyone was stretching, trying to loosen up. At 7:00 a.m. exactly, the gun went off and the mass entry into the water was absolute bedlam. As usual, I was in no hurry to join the melee!

By the time I decided to enter the lake there were probably 100 triathletes left on the shore. We had opted for the sane approach to the swim event and took a leisurely stroll to the water's edge before easing ourselves in. I planned, modestly, to beat the 2:20:00 cut-off time in this first part of the race. The Ironman Canada swim is one loop of the lake, no breaks along the way. I decided to follow another swimmer who was moving at about the same speed as I was so I didn't have to check my position all the time. My strategy worked and I arrived at the end of the loop inside the cut-off time! I must say I was glad to see the "strippers," who got me out of my wetsuit in a hurry.

The bike event also went well. I found my groove early, and the 180 km haul from Penticton to Osoyoos, over Richter Pass, on to Keremeos and back to Penticton was smooth. When I transitioned to the run, I had been working at the race for seven hours. Then came the marathon.

For the first half, I was still feeling great. Then the wheels come off.

Looking back now, I think the main reason the second half of the run was so difficult for me was the heat. In my endurance career I've learned that I'm better at -30°C rather than +30°. At sub-zero temperatures, I can layer up and prepare myself for the cold. But when the heat rises, my head cooks. The day of the Ironman was a particularly warm one, and I think I started my run at too fast a pace. Also, I probably wasn't hydrated enough after the bike event. When I hit the wall, my only objective was to finish the race in under 17 hours, the cut-off time. I ended up walking in with two other participants. I did run in the last 200 m and was cheered by the encouragement of so many people yelling and hooting on the sidelines. I crossed the line at 16:30:28.

The best part of an Ironman, I think, comes at the end, regardless of how you've done. The last stretch is lined with people – participants and family and friends – who are yelling and screaming, encouraging participants to get in under the 17:00:00 cut-off. I crossed the line and wrapped a silver blanket around myself to keep my body heat in. Then I went straight to the finish line aid station and started to eat and drink. The cheers of the sideline crowd got louder and louder as the clock moved toward midnight and the 17-hour cut-off. I could see the countdown clock from where I was eating at the station, and the crowd went crazy when a female runner came in with only two seconds to spare.

In the end, I was glad to have made it in before the cut-off, and even more pleased that Sue was there to help me back to the campground, where I slept like a log on my comfortable Thermarest.

I'm happy to say that my next big event wasn't quite as gruelling as Ironman Canada. On September 11, 2005, Sue and I were married. Her son Calum, dad Eric and my sister Sally flew over from the UK. Kristina and Autumn flew in from Sudbury and Peter and Helen came with my nephews, Jonathan and Christopher. Unfortunately, Sue's mum, Terryanne, was unable to make the journey, due to ill health. But we were determined she should be part of our special day. The simple service took place in our home and we set up the phone on speaker mode so that Terryanne could listen in. Calum gave Sue away and then we all set off for the Banff Springs Hotel and a celebratory meal. Sue and I soon settled down to married life.

6

MOVING UP TO ULTRAS

"If you start to feel good during an ultra,
don't worry, you will get over it."

—GENE THIBEAULT

When you think about ultramarathons and their participants, maybe you think about historical conditions: rocky paths, desert-like landscapes, couriers carrying their messages forward over days of hard terrain, intent on their goals; or maybe you consider modern-day ultra-distance racers with super-fit bodies and hard-as-nails attitudes to match the crazy courses set for them in races with tough names like Spartathon (Greece) and Badwater (United States). Or maybe you think about the underdogs, guys like Cliff Young, whose training involves rounding up sheep rather than carefully planned routes and training sessions. In 2008 I became an ultramarathoner. It just seemed to be the natural progression for me from Ironman events onward. I'm not sure which category I fit into of the above, probably none of them, but I do know I love ultra racing.

From 2006 to 2007 I solidified my post-retirement career in marathons and triathlons. I also needed to earn some money, so I started renovating houses and condos with my brother Peter. At the same time, Sue and I found another interest. We had seen an ad in the *Calgary Herald* seeking volunteers to appear in a movie that was being shot in the city. We enjoyed the experience and so decided to sign up with an agency that supplies extras for TV shows and movies. We had great fun and have appeared in some films and several episodes of *Heartland*.

In 2006, at the Kelowna Marathon, I qualified for the Boston Marathon with a time of 3:32:29. Throughout 2006 and 2007 I travelled from Stony Plain, Alberta, to Yellowknife, NWT, and then south to Las Vegas, in search of tris, marathons and half-Ironman events. At the Las Vegas half-marathon I accidently started the race in the corral with the elite runners. I don't think I've ever responded so quickly to a starter's pistol in my life! The highlight of those years, though, was my second Ironman Canada in August 2007, which I completed in 14:31:30, with a marathon time of 4:04:00 – much better than my 2005 attempt.

The year 2008, however, brought a change of direction. My friend and running club buddy Andrew started telling me about ultramarathons: running races whose distances are over 42.2 km. Usually ultras are 50 or 100 km and 50 or 100 mi. (80 or 160 km) in length – and they take place all over the world, from the Antarctic to New Zealand, South Africa to northern Alberta. I thought again about the late Cliff Young and his triumph in the Westfield Sydney to Melbourne Ultramarathon. I thought about the Cliff Young Australian Six-Day Race – an ultra named after Cliff which was run until 2006.

When I found myself thinking about how Cliff had persevered despite the odds and his age, and when I thought about how I loved a challenge, I knew I was interested. I had really been enjoying the Ironman races and longer tris, and I wanted to test myself. But first, I had to contend with a simpler race, the Boston Marathon.

My time in the 2006 Kelowna race had allowed me to qualify for another go-round in Boston. A group of us from Cochrane had qualified, so we all travelled south and east together. The day of the race dawned overcast and drizzling and our bus to the start at Hopkinton was late; we arrived with only two minutes to spare. Not a good beginning! Just as the pistol sounded, though, the sun came out. The run went well, and I came in at 4:12:42. I felt good, but because I had decided not to wear a hat or sunscreen – well, it did look as if it would be a rainy day at first – I developed a horrible sunburn that led to water collecting between skull and scalp on top of my head and down my forehead. Over the next few days, with an oddly blue, aloe-vera paste slathered all over my pate, I looked like a blue Herman Munster. A note to all runners out there: always bring a hat to a long race!

I felt pretty sorry for myself when I came home, but I couldn't mope around. I only had four weeks to train for my first ultramarathon: the 100 km Blackfoot Ultra at Cooking Lake Blackfoot Recreation Area east of Edmonton. I increased my training load in preparation for this race, and by the time I set out I had put in a number of 100 km weeks. This entailed several short runs during the week and a 40 km run on the weekend. I also completed back-to-back 30 km runs in order to get used to running on tired legs. Of course, I had to be prepared to run 100 km in one day, in this case four loops around the lovely Lost Lake.

Something all ultras have in common is the way in which they appeal to their participants. Extreme names like Scorched Sole, Knee Knackering North Shore Trail Run and the Canadian Death Race abound in lists of ultras – especially, it seems, in lists of Canadian races! The Canadian Death Race's logo is a skull with the tagline "It's a killer," not to mention the claim "There are no big prizes for winning, finishing is hard enough. And the bragging rights are priceless..." The Blackfoot Ultra is described thus: "If you are an optimist, all the hills will be good for tightening your butt. If you are a pessimist, well too bad, because the race director is an optimist and enjoy your new tight butt."

I was prepared for the worst, I thought. Having completed marathons and Ironman triathlons, I was interested in seeing how my first ultra experience would turn out. I had never run farther than 42.2 km at a time, so moving up to run 100 km in one event was a huge step.

What struck me most about the start of the Blackfoot Ultra was the low-key nature of the event. It began with a small group of runners gathered at the start line in the dark with headlamps on. An administrator asked if everyone was there. We all said, "Yes," but if someone was missing I'm not sure anyone would have noticed. We all shuffled out at a reasonable pace. It was going to be a long day, so nobody sprinted from the start. The course rolled around a series of lakes and was comprised of four 25 km loops. I found a good rhythm and took a sip out of my hydration pack every 10 minutes. My friends Wayne and Ken had introduced me to Carbo-Pro earlier in the year. This powder mixes in water and provides 300 calories an hour – I used Carbo-Pro during the Blackfoot race and many races after that.

As the sun came up, I spotted a flock of pelicans gathered on one of the lakes. When I hit the first aid station, I discovered a key difference between marathons and ultras. At marathon stations you get water, Gatorade, gels and, if you're lucky, a banana. At ultra stations you get real food. The Blackfoot stations served up potatoes, sandwiches, fruit and cookies.

As the hours wore on, I found myself in a semi-Zen state, which didn't last because I bashed my right big toe into a wooden plank on a bridge. I told myself to focus, but on the next lap I did the same thing to the other big toe. Still, I kept a steady pace and seemed to have achieved a hydration–nutrition balance. I've said it before and I'll say it again: I know that I'm lucky; I can eat and run and not have gastric problems.

At the end of each lap, Sue gave me support and a cup of home-made soup. When I finally came round to her after the final lap, my time was 13:38:23. Unlike at marathons and Ironman events there were no crowds lining the sides at the end and yelling encouragement, just a lady at a desk, writing down my finish time and telling me I could get a hotdog and popsicle over at the finish tent. It didn't matter to me, however, that I didn't come in to great whoops and cheers. The feeling of that race – the elation at running for such a long time, the mixed-up feeling of exhaustion and exhilaration at the end – stayed with me. I was hooked.

ULTRA-NUTRITION AND SUPER-GEAR

When I started running ultramarathons, some of the events had me competing for up to 35 continuous hours. Because of the length of time participants are running, these events have incredible aid stations. The big marathons usually lay out stations with energy drinks and silver blankets. At ultras, runners are regaled with high-protein, high-carbohydrate fuel: sometimes ice cream and hot dogs, sometimes salmon, pasta, potatoes, trays of bacon, brownies, cookies, fruit and coffee. When running an ultra, I carried a 3-litre hydration pack filled with water mixed with Carbo-Pro powder. Carbo-Pro is pure glucose polymers extracted from food grains. I found I had a hard time swallowing the energy gels during long races; they were too thick, and unpalatable.

The clothes I wore to ultras were also different than the ones I wore to marathons or tris. One of my key ultra-garments was my "Glad" rain jacket: a garbage bag with holes for head and arms. I wore the bag in between my shirt and jacket when it rained. It wouldn't keep me dry, but it ensured that I didn't lose heat from my core. Another key piece of gear was my Salomon XT Wings Gore-Tex trail shoes.

You know me by now! After the Blackfoot race, I was convinced about ultras. I signed up for the Canadian Death Race (August) and the Lost Soul Ultra (September). Both were gruelling, but for different reasons. The Canadian Death Race is a 125 km route across three mountain ranges near Grande Cache, Alberta. The Lost Soul takes the runner up and down, through the usually summer-parched coulees of Lethbridge, Alberta – three loops equal

100 miles. "The strenuous life tastes better," as the Lost Soul race director quoted William James, the father of American psychology. Maybe so. James certainly felt that strenuous living allowed people to contend with physical and psychological disabilities. Running shall set you free!

The Canadian Death Race would be the next step in my ultra-marathon career. This race has been going since 2000 and begins and ends on a 1280 m plateau, crosses the Smoky and Sulphur rivers at Hell's Gate, passes over three mountain summits and includes 5182 m of elevation change. You can enter with a relay team or individually, but either way you push yourself to the limit!

Sue and I travelled up to Grand Cache and arrived about midday on Friday. After we dropped off our stuff at the motel, we headed down to the race package pickup. Lots of Death Racers were milling around, and at 5:00 p.m. the race information meeting was held. The MC was dressed like Darth Maul and he warned us all about the challenges of the 125 km trek.

That night, I slept badly, and in the morning it took me a couple cups of coffee to get my head in the game. I shuffled down to the start line at 8:00 a.m. and the gun went off. The race is five legs. The first, Downtown Jaunt, is 19 km. This is a warm-up to the 27 km Flood Mountain and Grande Mountain section. There were parts of this route that were so steep and muddy that I was grabbing at trees and branches to keep my balance on the way down. Section three, the 21 km Old Mine Road part, was a bit of a break, but then came section four, the 36 km Hamel Assault, which was the toughest part the course.

The route took us to the top of Mount Hamel, and for a few brief moments I stopped and slowly turned 360 degrees, just to take in the view. Then we headed down and into the valley. By this time it was dark, and I was thrilled to see Sue at the start of the last section, the 24 km River Crossing. She fed me cheese and ham sandwiches and a mug of chicken noodle soup – heaven. Five minutes later I was off again. I was dead tired and dragging myself along the trail. It was my first all-night run, and I kept seeing shadows and hearing noises just outside the field of vision of my headlamp.

Soon I was on Hell's Gate Road, heading toward the Smoky River. Here I had to dig out the coin I had been given at the race package pickup and give it to the Ferryman. No coin, no passage across the river. During the final 10 km, the sun rose above the horizon. The warmth gave me a new lease on life, and I picked up the pace toward the finish line. The cut-off time was 24 hours, and I came in at 22:52:40.

Sue was at the finish line waiting for me with a bottle of Guinness and a big hug. A new tradition thus began. Sue would support me throughout races, being at the aid stations, often having to find her way in the dark, carrying all the provisions I would need at various stages. These would include changes of clothing, food and fuel refills. After an ultra she would always have amusing stories to tell about the things she saw and heard while waiting for me to come in.

At one such race a young guy had both his parents at one of the stations, ready with a chair, blankets, a hot meal and lots of TLC. As he sat down and began complaining about the cold, a woman racer breezed through the camp and, upon hearing him, called out, "Suck it up, Princess!" and without even stopping she continued on to the next section.

Sometimes, though, waiting wasn't fun. Sue would spend long periods just worrying, never knowing quite where I was on the route, whether I would be in during the next few minutes or even hours, or if I was injured or lost, and dealing with comments from other racers like, "I've just seen two grizzlies beside the path!" There are times when I wonder if it's harder being support crew or racing. When you're racing, at least you know where you are, most of the time!

With Sue as support, I felt I could get through any race. Still, after the Death Race, the Lost Soul hundred-miler in September was a difficult one. Things went well for the first 65 km, then all hell broke loose. At 6:00 p.m. a thunderstorm crossed the coulees, hitting the dry land with torrential rain. The clay trail couldn't absorb the amount of water that poured down, and soon we runners were slipping and sliding all over the place. My pace dropped to 2 km an hour, and at 11:00 p.m. the race director called the whole thing off due to safety considerations. Some of the route markers had been washed away and some runners were getting lost. Of course, I didn't know the race was off right away. My lasting memory of this race is of me sliding down a hill in the dark through pouring rain and sighting a glowing tent in the valley. When I walked into the warmth of that tent and was told that the race was cancelled, I experienced one of the happiest moments of my life.

After my foray into ultras in 2008, my plans were pretty simple at the beginning of 2009. I scheduled myself in for a number of ultras: a 50 km race in February in Calgary called the Frozen Ass Fifty; a 44 km snowshoe race in March in Yellowknife called the Rock and Ice Ultra; a 146 km trail race called the Sinister Seven in the Crowsnest Pass, BC; and again the Lost Soul Ultra in September. As well, Sue had also begun running at this point, and I wanted us to do a half-marathon together.

Over the winter of 2008–2009, I spent much of my training time at Middle Lake in Kananaskis Country, running a 1 km loop on the frozen water. With repeated visits, I slowly carved a groove hugging the shoreline. Through January and February I built up to 30 km per session out at the lake – and every time I went there the landscape was different. A new layer of snow may have fallen, or perhaps the wind had sculpted the existing snow and ice into strange shapes. I followed my groove through the snow, feeling strong, clear-headed, ready for a year of challenges.

7
RIGHT TO PLAY

"Look after yourself, look after one another."

—RIGHT TO PLAY

Oh, I had found my calling in running. I was moving from one goal to the next, enjoying the training, feeling the satisfaction that comes with each race, revelling in each triumph and learning from each disappointment. But there was something missing. I had brought play back into my life, but it was time to turn my play into something that would benefit others. Tom helped me see that. And Right To Play came into my life.

In early February, after returning from another 30 km around Middle Lake, I checked my e-mail and found a message from an old friend, Michael. He and I had worked together at the Con gold mine in Yellowknife back in the early 1980s and we had stayed in touch. He wrote to let me know that Tom – my old boss (and a great guy) at the Sullivan Mine in Kimberley – was in Calgary, and passed along his phone number, suggesting that I drop him a line. I hadn't thought about Tom in a long time and I was keen to get back in touch.

Later that evening, I called Tom and he asked me over to dinner the next night. The moment I walked in the door I could tell Tom had a plan. We talked for a while about our common interest in running and skiing. Then he sat me down and told me about Right To Play.

I had already heard a little bit about the organization. I remembered when speed skater and cyclist Clara Hughes donated $10,000 to RTP in 2006. I remember thinking Clara must have felt pretty strongly about RTP to take this action. She did. She was behind Right To Play 100 per cent and has since talked a lot about RTP's

Three boys having fun with their wooden scooters on a road in Tanzania.

ability to make change happen by helping children in dire circumstances build leadership and peacemaking skills, learn about healthy habits and gain self-confidence, all through games and sport. As I listened to Tom talk about RTP with the enthusiasm I had seen him display so many times before, I wondered what he was getting at.

While we were eating dinner, Tom made a statement I wouldn't soon forget: "Their idea isn't to feed a bunch of bellies – that doesn't solve anything. Right To Play is in 20-some different countries, and they've designated coaches to teach about the importance of inclusiveness. They've also implemented programs for kids to play while learning to respect one another, so they can grow up and turn into future leaders as well."

Slowly he came around to his point. Tom wanted to know if I would be interested in doing something to raise funds for RTP, run some races, get some donations. I must admit I was drawn to his suggestion right away. There was something about RTP's mandate that captured me. I suppose I didn't know it at that point, but the idea of play – in my case running, biking, racing – allowing a person to grow and change and become stronger is as much a part of my story as it is RTP's. And my cycling trip from Cairo to the Cape had shown me the power of sport in children's lives, from the soccer mania to the roadside table tennis, the kids were keen to play. What would happen if an organization embraced playfulness and made it part of a program that helped kids help themselves and their communities?

Although Tom's spiel already had me hooked, I took a couple of days to think about it and to read more about RTP. I decided to do some research. Right To Play's history spoke for itself.

I was really taken by the organization's approach, and its motto: "Look after yourself, look after one another." By training local coaches to run its programs, RTP encourages a long-term presence of sport and play programming in communities. For example, in 2009 I found out that RTP was establishing an initiative in Benin by

Running marathon #141 with Kathy and Robin around MacKay's ice cream store in Cochrane, Alberta.

RIGHT TO PLAY: A SHORT HISTORY

Right To Play began as Olympic Aid in 1994, the brainchild of the Lillehammer Olympic Organizing Committee (LOOC). Originally, Olympic Aid was to focus on supporting people in war-torn countries, with Olympic athletes working as ambassadors to assist in raising money. The lead athlete ambassador was Norwegian speed skater Johann Olav Koss, who donated a great deal of his Olympic winnings to Olympic Aid and challenged others to do the same. As a result of Koss's endeavour, Olympic Aid raised $18-million, which went to five big projects in 1994, including a hospital in Sarajevo, schools in Eritrea and a mother–child program in Guatemala.

The organization continued to raise money for children in dire situations between 1994 and 2000. Projects included a joint venture with UNICEF which funnelled $13-million raised before and after the Atlanta Olympics to a vaccination program that benefited 12.2 million kids and more than 800,000 women. The effort resulted in temporary "Olympic Truces" in Afghanistan and the Kurdish region in northern Iraq, where fighting ceased in order to allow UNICEF staff to immunize the women and children.

By late 2000 Olympic Aid had incorporated and become Right To Play, no longer a "fundraising vehicle" but a non-governmental organization (NGO). Beginning in March 2001, RTP started implementing sport and play programs, the first ones in refugee communities in Angola and Côte d'Ivoire.

As RTP found its legs as an NGO, it began hosting roundtables about sport relative to development issues like HIV and AIDS prevention, health and refugee rehabilitation. Such roundtables have been attended by the likes of then-UN Secretary-General Kofi Annan, Archbishop Desmond Tutu, Dr. Jacques Rogge, Steven Lewis and others, who helped place sport and development on the international agenda.

Today, Right To Play maintains its position as a leader in the field of sport for development. It advocates for every child's right to play and is active in trying to turn that right into a reality for kids the world over. Right To Play's vision is to "engage leaders on all sides of sport, business and media to ensure every child's right to play."

RIGHT TO PLAY'S METHOD

It's about playing, but there's a method to the play! RTP's ultimate goal in delivering sport programs to kids is to effect positive behavioural change, which involves kids acquiring the knowledge and attitude they need to gain and maintain self-esteem, peaceful conflict-resolution skills, problem-solving skills, communication techniques and resistance to peer pressure. Right To Play recognizes that in order to support kids on their journey to acquiring these skills, someone must be there to create and maintain supportive environments, help the kids develop life skills and healthy attitudes, and guide them toward acquiring knowledge about local and world issues. Once it is established in a community, RTP aims to encourage that supportive environment by enlisting the help of community members to be role models and supporters of change. The organization then sets to work in helping kids and communities change, through programs of repetitive sport and play, guiding them from kids who *are unaware* of their ability to be community advocates to kids who *are* community advocates.

RTP customizes its programming based on community needs, providing games and programs that are relevant. And the results are fantastic!

THE ROCK AND ICE ULTRA

The Rock and Ice Ultra is a crazy set of three events, a race that *Canadian Geographic* calls "one of the most demanding endurance races in the Far North." The first event is the six-day Diamond Ultramarathon, a 225 km unsupported foot and snowshoe or cross-country ski race. Each competitor must pull a pulk – a low-slung toboggan – carrying all his or her food and gear. Participants come from all over the world for this event, not just for the purse – diamonds donated by sponsor BHP Billiton – but for the intensity and the glory that comes with being able to say you've pulled a pulk through the Diamond Ultra. Of course, not everyone who enters makes it through; in 2007, during the first Diamond Ultra, about two-thirds of the runners didn't finish the race.

The second event is the K-Rock Ultramarathon, a three-day, 135 km supported race over the same kind of terrain I raced through in the third event – the 44 km Cold Foot Classic – frozen lakes and taiga. Let's just say the whole endeavour is not for the faint of heart! The race has not been held since 2009, but hopefully it will make a comeback.

working with the nation's Ministry of Education and establishing programs at 15 different sites in the country. But Benin was just the tip of the iceberg: RTP operated 48 projects in 23 countries in 2009. I was impressed.

At the end of the week, I called Tom to tell him I was in. We spent February and March planning how we would organize ourselves. We contacted Robert Witchel, Canadian national director of RTP, and let him know what we were thinking about. Firsts we set a fundraising target: $10,000, à la Clara Hughes! We also decided to encourage friends and family to join us in our quest. We called ourselves Kids-U-Can and, with the help of our friend Jeffrey, set up a website. Our first event would be the Vancouver Half-marathon, scheduled for early May.

In the meantime, my racing schedule progressed. I had already run the Frozen Ass Fifty, so my next event was the Rock and Ice Ultra in Yellowknife in mid-March. This race had three events, and I would be competing in the third: the Cold Foot Classic, a one-day 44 km snowshoe and run, or cross-country ski, race across frozen lakes and taiga (the northern coniferous forest belt in between the treeless tundra to the north and the boreal forest to the south).

The Cold Foot Classic was scheduled for a day when the temperature was a biting −35°c. All my cold-weather training came into play; I knew I could survive the race. As we lined up at the start, I must admit I wondered about a couple of the competitors. They had pieces of duct tape on their cheeks and across their noses to protect them from frost bite. This was a new one to me (and it didn't work out very well for them). At 7:00 a.m. the gun went off and a colourful array of runners, snowshoers and cross-country skiers headed across the lake. I was wearing double gloves and a balaclava and was equipped with hand warmers. I also had my Atlas "Race" snowshoes, so I was in good shape. I kissed Sue goodbye and hammered out.

I felt good and kept a good pace for the first 30 km, up until the first aid station, which was in a tent. I ducked into the tent with clear skies above me and came out a few minutes later straight into a whiteout. The trail was marked with pink ribbon every 100 m, which worked well when it was clear. Not anymore. Now, volunteers had to infill every 50 m with ribbon, just so the runners could stay on track.

Progress was brutally slow, and at one point I lost all sense of direction. I couldn't see ribbon in front or behind me. The trail seemed to end right where my snowshoes left off and I had no idea where I was. For several minutes I just stood on the trail, rooted to the ground. I didn't see much point in moving, as I had no idea in which direction to head. So I stood and listened. The silence was deafening. Then I heard a call: two female cross-country skiers had spotted me. I joined their convoy and continued on my way. Soon we were out of the clouds and I crossed the line at 7:08:00. Incredibly, and happily, I was the winner of the Cold Foot Classic snowshoe section.

Back in Calgary the planning for Kids-U-Can continued. By late April we had 40 members and $2,000 had been donated to RTP. Sue and I travelled to Vancouver for the half-marathon and met Tom and his friend Cyrus. We had a total of 35 members either running the full, half- or 8 km race. Tom, Cyrus, Sue and I raced the half, and by the end of the day the donations stood at $3,500. The members initially planned to participate in nine events in 2009, but by the end of the year the roster had grown to over 20 races.

It didn't take long before we had 50 fellow runners signed up to help out; in the end our loose "team" consisted of over 100 members. We selected a number of races – from 5 and 10 km runs to marathons and ultramarathons – as the core fundraisers for the cause. I say "core" because those who joined us added their own races to the mix; one of our team members, Ken, raised money for RTP while running in the Great Tibetan Marathon in

Ladakh, India, that July, and the Istanbul Marathon in October. Another member, Paul, ran the Portland Marathon in Australia in November.

As the year went on, my races got longer. After Yellowknife, I ran the Sinister Seven in July. This is a 146 km trail run through the mountains in the Crowsnest Pass in southern BC. This one was a killer. I got wet feet after 13 hours of running and made the mistake of not stopping to put on dry socks. When I finished, my feet were like pancakes. A layer of skin fell off when I removed my soaking socks. Still, I finished in 26:41:19, 20 minutes inside the 27-hour cut-off time.

My next race was the Edmonton Marathon, but in my mind I was already past that and preparing for the Lost Soul in September. After being rained out in 2008, I was determined to give that ultra a good shot in 2009! In training, I was running up to three marathons a week, and I was feeling good.

It was as I prepared for the Lost Soul race that a germ of an idea entered my brain. I was really enjoying running the races I wanted to run and at the same time fundraising for Right To Play, but something told me I could do more.

One evening in late June, after my third marathon of the week, I came home and told Sue that I had an idea and wanted to run 365 marathons in 2010 as a fundraiser for Right To Play. She looked at me, paused and told me to go see my doctor. Somehow, I knew going to see Dr. Bill Hanlon wouldn't throw a wrench into my plans. Bill had climbed the seven highest peaks on the seven continents, including Mount Everest, and he later skied to the South Pole. Instead of receiving a warning or a flat-out no from Dr. Hanlon, we had a good chat and came up with the very sensible idea of running five marathons a week, or 262 in total, instead. This way, I would have two recovery days per week, allowing me room to breathe. In the end, we dropped the total marathons down to 250, which allowed me 12 spare days for unforeseen events.

ATHLETE AMBASSADOR FOR RIGHT TO PLAY: BECKIE SCOTT

I met Beckie in 2009 when she was Western Canada Coordinator for Right To Play activities. As I prepared for Marathon Quest 250, Beckie gave me lots of support. Beckie is one of Canada's most successful cross-country skiers, and one of the best in the world. She won two Olympic medals: gold at the 2002 Salt Lake City Games and silver with Sara Renner at the 2006 games in Torino. She retired in 2006 and has been an active advocate of fair play and drug-free sport – she is currently serving an eight-year term with the IOC's Athletes' Commission from 2006 to 2014. But Beckie doesn't limit her activities to the sports world: she also gives to the community through sport. She has worked with UNICEF as a special representative, and she joined Right To Play as an athlete ambassador in 2003.

RTP Athlete Ambassadors serve as role models for kids all over the world by taking part in programs, travelling to program locations and speaking to the media on behalf of Right To Play, which helps the organization raise money. Beckie has travelled with Right To Play around Canada, and she has taken part in programs in Ethiopia.

I went home and told Sue that 250 marathons were just what the doctor ordered. A week later I headed over to Tom's place and told him my plan. He said, "Go for it!" The rest of the year was a blur. In August I ran the Edmonton Marathon and Calum came over from England and ran his first half-marathon. In September I ran the Lost Soul with my buddy Andy, and we completed it in 35:18:42, just over 40 minutes inside the 36-hour cut-off time. After that I spent a month putting together an operating manual for the event we were calling Marathon Quest 250.

In October Tom and I headed over to Toronto to present the idea to Right To Play. I'll always remember sitting with Tom in the lobby of the One King West Hotel in downtown Toronto. Robert from RTP sat facing us as I made the pitch for the fundraiser. He was quiet at first. Nothing was said for about 30 seconds – and that's a long time when you are waiting for a response. Then he said Right To Play would support me, and we shook hands.

After getting the go-ahead from Robert, I spent November and December gathering strength. In the middle of November I made a presentation to Cochrane Town Council to garner their support, and the two local papers, the *Eagle* and the *Times*, reported the story. I told them I planned to cover a distance of 10,550 km. The majority of my marathons would be in the Cochrane–Calgary area, but the distance would be equivalent to my running from Cochrane east to Montreal, then south to Boston, then west through the U.S. to Seattle, up to Vancouver and back to Cochrane. I also let them know I would be doing one marathon a week at a school, and that I would be working with the Rotary Club of Cochrane to place maps of my virtual cross country route in local schools so that kids could feel involved and be able to comprehend the distance covered. I was touched by the support I received from council. Mayor Truper McBride was behind me all the way, saying, "It's an incredible undertaking." I didn't know what to say, but I thanked them, happy to have them behind me.

I soon received calls from news media in Calgary, and within a week CNN wanted an interview. Tony Harris interviewed me at the end of December – he had the same response to my idea that most people had at the time: "Are you nuts, 250 marathons next year? Really?" I answered, "I could be, Tony. It has been said before." But really, Tony was supportive; he checked in with me at the end of 2010 as well, and was cheerful and encouraging. I was confident in my plan, but it helped to have the reassurance given to me by others, close to home and abroad.

Of course, not everyone was encouraging. As I embarked on the quest, I read my fair share of discouragement in the news media. But I always tried to dismiss it.

During the last part of 2009 I picked a marathon route from my house that covered roads in the foothills. Marcel LaMontagne from Athletics Canada offered to come out and measure an official course for free, which was fortunate. There is a set procedure for the measurement and authorizing of a marathon course. Marcel spent a day measuring the course twice using a special bike: a mechanical counter is located between the front forks and wheel. After all the paperwork was done, I received a certificate for the "Cochrane Foothills Marathon" course, what I would call the Horse Creek Loop.

Another item I needed to confront before the New Year hit was less glamorous, but necessary: I needed to ensure I had enough money to allow me to run. I figured the quest would cost me $50,000 to complete.

Although Sue was working, we had no real savings and I would be "unemployed" for a year. I had to find a way to help me cover some of the basic items I would need if I were to have any chance of being successful. It became a matter of approaching everyone I could think of with pleas for help. It soon became clear that many people were skeptical about me reaching my goal, and others were unprepared to cover me for the long term. It was with great relief that some brave individuals and companies had more faith and were prepared to take a chance on me, step forward and donate to my operating budget. In the end, 40 sponsors donated a total of $43,000 of in-kind products to help me through. I was so grateful to have their support. I can honestly say I would not have completed my quest without it.

Two products I used during the quest deserve a special mention. The first is Back on Track recovery apparel, which helped me especially during the cold months and when I was injured. The other is Carbo-Pro, which sustained me and provided vital nutrition throughout the year, and was generously donated by Ferg Hawke. Ferg has an incredible story of his own: this Air Canada baggage handler is an amazing ultrarunner. I would recommend anyone, runner or not, to see the movie *The Distance of Truth*, in which his run in the Badwater ultra is featured.

During the last two weeks of December, despite all the support and cooperation of my teammates, some uncertainty crept in. I had to keep telling myself I could do it. Sue, Tom, Cyrus, Jeffrey, Lyn, Adam and I made a great team. Each person played a key role. Sue – as always, my greatest support – was lining up schools for my Thursday marathons. Tom was looking for other running venues; Jeffrey had the website up and running; Lyn was handling all the PR issues; Cyrus made video; and Adam was on the lookout for sponsors. In the meantime, Kids-U-Can ended the year with 100 members, and by December 31, we had raised the $10,000 we had hoped for. I had no reason to be nervous – Kids-U-Can had been successful. There was every reason to think that Marathon Quest 250 would also find its way. But Kids-U-Can was a team of people; Marathon Quest 250, no matter how many people ran marathons with me, was my own effort. I worried.

On the night of December 31, 2009, I checked the weather report for the next day with my marathon in mind: –32°c. I wondered why I hadn't picked a warmer location for the quest – San Diego, perhaps?

THE DONATIONS

I could not have made it through 2010 without the donations from the following companies and individuals.

COMPANY	ACTIVITY	IN KIND VALUE
ANT+	wireless	$2,500
Arc of the Universe	music	$530
Back on Track	therapeutic clothing	$650
Cadence PR	public relations	$2,500
Calgary Marathon	registration	$80
Carbo-Pro	run nutrition	$4,250
Cochrane Awards	T-shirts and coat	$820
Cochrane Fitness	fitness gym	$580
Cochrane Sport Physio	physio, VO_2 max testing and RMR	$3,450
Copper Chimney	restaurant	$1,000
Course Measurement	certify courses	$2,000
Dynastream	running data	$1,000
Eau Claire YMCA	passes	$100
Edge Sports	sports gear	$300
Cochrane Eagle	newspaper	$100
Fast Trax Run & Ski Shop	sports gear	$300
Fit Foods	food	$350
Footstock Race Weekend	registration	$70
Gord's Running Store	shoes	$180
Hotel Soleil	Vancouver Marathon	$450
Hot Stone Massage	massage	$480

Impact Magazine	shoes	$510
Kyle and Joe's Lemonade Stand	lemonade	$20
Kodesign	architect models	$2,500
MacKay's	ice cream	$280
Mainstreet Pharmacy	medical	$40
Mountain View Optometry	sunglasses	$150
New Balance Store	shoes	$400
Parachute Web Design	MQ 250 website	$2,500
ProActive Health	chiropractic / massage	$2,400
Professional Coaches	shoes	$190
Rotary Club of Cochrane	virtual map	$1,500
Rurbanlens	videography	$1,000
Salomon	trail shoes	$750
Speed Theory	electrolytes	$225
Speed Matrix	fundraising	$2,500
Strides	running shoes	$180
The Tech Shop	running shoes	$250
TrakkersGPS	real-time running data	$1,000
Trailblazers	outdoor gear	$930
USANA	supplements	$2,020
Vancouver Marathon	registration	$90
WestJet	flights	$1,500
Woody's Marathon	registration	$130

LEARNING TO COOPERATE THE RTP WAY: CIRCLE UP

When you are on a team, it is important to cooperate in order to play well, avoid conflict and succeed. RTP's Circle Up game teaches cooperation.

Kids form a large, standing circle. Each child in the circle must remember the names of the people to their left and right. Once this is accomplished, the kids are then asked to reform the circle, standing side by side in the alphabetical order of their names. They have to reorganize themselves as quickly as possible. When done, they each call out their names in order. Then they re-form the original circle and call out the name of the person on their right.

When the game is over, the RTP coach encourages kids to reflect on what they've learned by playing the game and helping one another. Some leaders may have emerged during the course of the game, but the coach reminds all of the kids to connect with what they've learned about their own potential to become leaders. Developing cooperation skills allows kids to build on their leadership potential.

8

WINTER: NOW THAT'S COLD

"It hurts up to a point and it doesn't get any worse."
—ANN TRASON, ultrarunner

I began Marathon Quest 250 in the depths of winter, just when most people would prefer to be sitting at home, cozy in front of a roaring fire, enjoying a good book perhaps. I launched myself into my routine with the kind of forward movement that wouldn't allow me a moment to rethink my decision. "I would complete this quest," I thought, "regardless of the weather!"

At 8:30 a.m. on January 1, Sue and I left the house. Before starting the 15-minute, 1 km walk north to Highway 1A, Sue took the first of what would become known as the "First Light" pictures. Every day she would take a photo of me standing next to the tree outside our house. Over the course of the year, they showed the changes in the seasons and how I had dressed for the varying weather conditions.

As we set off, a full moon hovered over the mountains and the sun was coming up. It was −30°C, a bit warmer than predicted. I had suited up in my full winter running gear for Marathon 001, but as we made our way to the start, the fluid in my CamelBak was already starting to freeze.

When we arrived at Highway 1A and Horse Creek Road, a group of friends from the Cochrane Red Rock Running & Tri Club were there waiting for me. They had decided to run the first marathon with me, and I was pleased to see that the temperature hadn't stopped them. Mayor Truper McBride and some other town councillors were also there, as were news reporters from the Cochrane *Times* and *Eagle* and crews from CTV and CBC. Mayor McBride said a few words and Sue took a bunch a photos. In one of them, my five running mates and I smiled madly for the camera. My friends were smiling because they

The four seasons of Marathon Quest 250.

had one marathon to run and were feeling excited at the start line. I was smiling because that is what you do when someone says, "Say cheese!" Even now, when I look at that photo, I remember what I was really thinking: "What the hell am I doing?"

Despite the cold, the first marathon went well and we crossed the finish line at 2:30 p.m. I was grateful for the company I had that

WINTER RUNNING GEAR

What does one wear to survive −30°C temperatures for six hours at a time? From bottom to top:

FEET: Salomon trail shoes, wool socks

LEGS: shorts, long johns, winter running tights (sometimes more than one layer of tights)

TORSO: nip guards (essential), short-sleeved top, merino long-sleeved shirt, wicking long-sleeved shirt, windproof shell, MQ 250 singlet

HEAD: beanie, woollen Canada toque, mask, two Buff neck warmers, sunglasses

HANDS: woollen gloves, mitts, hand warmers.

And then, what does one carry?

CAMELBAK: 3 litres of water mixed with Carbo-Pro (1,500 calories for five to six hours)

PACK: extra pair of socks, hand warmers, emergency toilet paper, three garbage bags with arm and neck holes, Band-Aids and my front-door key.

BELT: pouch with electrolyte tablets (three per hour of running), cell phone, camera and bear whistle (one can never be too careful in the foothills).

first day. The solo marathons I would run during the quest were often lonely, especially on cold winter days. So began the start of the routine I would set myself for the rest of the year: run, hot tub, blog, eat, sleep.

Alberta winters can be unforgivingly cold and windy, especially where I live in Cochrane. Of course, chinook winds would sometimes blow in over the Rockies and provide some respite, but most of my January and February runs were chilly. Even some of the March ones were icy, and the cold caused problems. In the beginning, I had to figure out how to manage a freezing hydration pack nozzle and hose to the bladder. "The product of the season" award went to the lowly hand warmer. I used 20 pairs during the month of January alone. I found that by popping two hand warmers into a zipper pouch and putting the nozzle of my pack into that warm nest, I had sort of solved my problem. For a while, I figured I really had a good product idea going there: the Nozzle Warmer-upper. I still need to work on the branding, of course.

I ran most of my initial marathons in Cochrane along the new Cochrane Foothills Marathon course. For me, each of the runs came in at around 51,000 steps. I would run down the 1A, then up Grand Valley Road past an area called the Wildcat Hills, which for some reason always sent shivers up my spine. An old steer at the George Fox homestead would eyeball me as I plodded past kilometre 19. After crossing RR 280, I would head down Horse Creek Road to the finish. There always seemed to be a murder of crows appraising me along this stretch. At kilometre 34 I fondly greeted the llamas, three of them, which were usually out in their pasture: two adults and a baby I started calling Titch. And at kilometre 40, just before I finished up, the same three horses and a donkey would look up and watch me pass.

During the course of Marathon Quest 250, I spoke to a few different reporters, updating them on my progress. At one point that winter, Mary-Catherine McIntosh from CBC wanted to know what I thought about as I ran. I told her I thought about food! A marathon course provides one with a good amount of time to think. Prior to Marathon Quest, I ran with ultrarunner Dean Karnazes, and he told me he used a Dictaphone as he ran in order to organize his thoughts toward writing a book. I did buy a Dictaphone, but by the time Mary-Catherine asked her question, I had only read to page three of the 16-page manual: very complicated. My main thoughts while running were about the information I would write in my daily blogpost.

I realized I needed to switch up my route a little bit every once in a while to avoid boredom, so for a while I ran the Cochrane Foothills Marathon course in the reverse direction once a week. The first time felt difficult, probably because the first 10 km was a long uphill grind and it didn't get better after that. The llamas were certainly surprised to see me so early in the day! After an hour or so, I felt drained and was questioning my decision to alter my direction, but runners Frank, Karen and Jody joined me at 30 km and their presence gave me a boost.

By the end of January I was in the groove, although some days were a bit weird. When you have a TV reporter and cameraman in

THE BEST BOND

I didn't tell Mary-Catherine this, but one of the thoughts that ran through my head as I ran the marathon course that winter was: who was the best James Bond? I felt it was appropriate to run a true test, beginning with the question of which Bond has run a marathon. Turns out Sean Connery ran the Rome Marathon in 2004, and I couldn't find running stats for any of the others. Sean Connery is therefore the best Bond. Who knew that question would be so easy to answer?

your kitchen at 6:30 a.m., life can hardly be called "normal." When Sue came out to get her first cup of coffee for the day, she was mighty glad to be wearing her pjs! She'd been used to runners turning up for coffee and the washroom before joining me to run, but that wasn't usually until 7-ish.

I'd become pretty relaxed about things by the end of January, accustomed to the early mornings and long hours. So much so that I didn't shrink from attending a Robbie Burns night put on by the Men of Vision Pipe & Drum Band, a fundraiser to help the band participate in a festival in Scotland. A key part of the evening was addressing the haggis, and after this was done we all tucked into a plate of the Scottish delicacy and mashed potatoes. I'd never carbo-loaded on haggis before, and I joked that it wasn't half "baaaaad." Of course, the next morning, a Sunday, I was rethinking my haggis revelry of the night before. My stomach was a little delicate as I walked up to the start line at 8:30! But I had the camaraderie of my running club mates to keep me going. Sundays had grown to be a Cochrane Running Club day, and I could always count on a few to come out and join me if I were running the Cochrane course. Unfortunately, by mid-February the novelty had worn off and I was on my own.

If ever I needed motivation to continue through the winter cold, I got it as January closed with an amazing marathon at Cambrian Heights School in Calgary. The morning of January 28, I ran Marathon 021, but before I started running I addressed the kids. As we walked to the gym, vice-principal Wendy and principal Bonnie showed me a wall across from the office that featured a life-sized cut-out of me with the outline of Calgary in the background.

At the assembly, I was introduced to cub reporter Norman, from Grade 3, who would follow me during the run and make a documentary of the day. He asked if he could have an exclusive interview and I of course agreed.

I started my run at 9:10 and put in 7 km in the first hour with a

MOTIVATIONAL PHRASES FROM AXE

As I made my way through the months of marathons, I tested many an interesting product, partly because a friend of mine, Mark, owns Trailblazers, a camping and outdoor store in Cochrane. He was gracious enough to help me out with some gear for the quest. In January alone, he had given me two boxes of hand warmers, a pair of gloves, four pairs of socks and a very special pair of sunglasses. The glasses were made by Axe, a Japanese company, and the copy on its packaging was incredibly motivational: "One step forward, for victory in your hand," "Superior technology to be sure of a great landing." If those phrases don't put zip into your step, I'm not sure what will!

JILLIAN SANBORNE'S GREAT IDEA

Jillian Sanborne celebrated her eighth birthday on January 2, and instead of asking for gifts, she requested that her friends and family to make donations to Right To Play. Three hundred dollars was donated in Jillian's name. I was impressed with Jillian's gift to the cause, and throughout the year, I continued to be impressed with kids' interest in what I was doing, and the work of Right To Play. I gave Jillian a poster, a certificate and the run number (008) of the day she had her birthday. Her interest in Marathon Quest also led her school, Elizabeth Barrett, to invite me to run on-site on June 24.

loop around the school, at which point Norman arrived and asked if I was ready to be interviewed. How could I say no? He took me to the staff room and asked me to sit on the comfy sofa. Four other Grade 3s took photos and video as Norman began: "What's your name?" "What's your favourite food?" "Do you have a pet?" "Who's your favourite friend?" The questions came thick and fast over the course of about 10 minutes, and Norman didn't back off. The other kids at Cambrian were just as precocious, and I chatted with them as I did my 50 loops around the school.

What a difference a change of month makes! February started off with 11°c temperatures with a touch of a warm chinook wind. By this time, I had begun including an avatar of myself on my blog: Avatar "Marathon Martin", a cut-out of me making a virtual tour on a route across North America and back. By February 1, my avatar had made it to Regina.

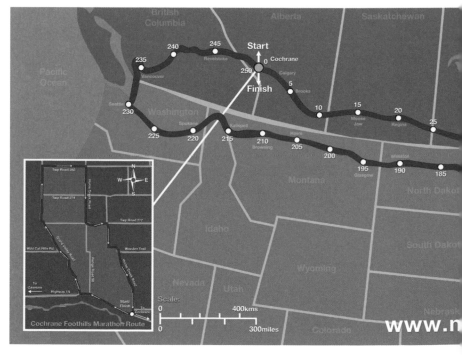

Avatar "Marathon Martin's" virtual route across North America.

By the time I ran at Marion Carson School in Calgary on February 10, I'd run 30 marathons in 41 days. Unfortunately, at this point, I had also developed the first of my marathon-related ailments.

The day before was a snowshoe marathon, which was fantastic but ended poorly when I had to walk the last 7 km because of shin pain. As I addressed the kids at Marion Carson, I worried that I would experience the same problem again that day. We all went out and did a winter walk, then I started the marathon. After 27 km, I was reduced to walking again. Advil didn't help. By the last kilometre, which I walked with the kids around the gym to the sound of The

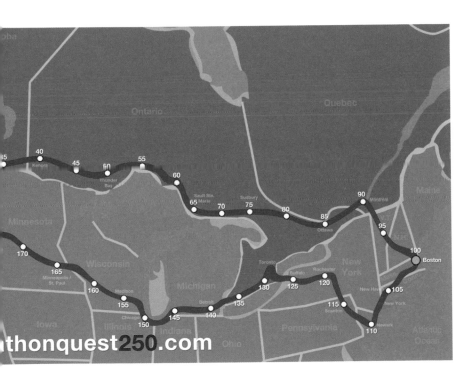

Proclaimers' "I'm Gonna Be (500 Miles)," I was fighting severe pain.

The next day, Dr. Hanlon sent me for an isotope bone scan and advised me to take a week off to wait for the results, using up some spare days I had in the bank. In the meantime, I did some physiotherapy with Serge Tessier at Cochrane Sports Physio. Serge had been giving me advice since December 2009, when he first conducted a baseline VO_2 max test, establishing my endurance level. When I went back to him in February, he tried to ascertain whether my shin problem was related to a stress fracture. It didn't seem so, but we couldn't be sure. He instructed me to do a few different stretches, gave my leg a hot–cold bath and finished me off with electrode stimulus to the muscle along the side of my bad shin. After that, I felt pretty good, at least until the next day when Dr. Hanlon gave me the results of my scan, which seemed to suggest I had a stress fracture. Talk about throwing a hammer in the works!

After some more poking around, however, Dr. Hanlon figured it was possible that I didn't have a fracture after all, and he sent me to see Dr. Kelly Brett at the Sports Medicine Clinic in Calgary. Fortunately for me, Dr. Brett decided that what I had was in fact repetitive strain injury to the muscles alongside the shin. This seemed like something I could face, but I still needed to make a rehab plan.

While all this was happening, I had time to reflect on what drove me to accept Tom's invitation to raise money for Right To Play in the first place the year before. I was looking back on my diary entries from the Tour d'Afrique, remembering the kids and their soccer balls and league talk, their table tennis and interest in the bike tour. This childish enthusiasm, this energy, can motivate kids to do good things within their families and communities, but it can also be directed toward violence or irresponsible behaviour. Of course, that amazing enthusiasm can also easily be stamped out by poverty, illness, violence or upheaval in a child's community.

I thought about Right To Play, its programs based on sport and physical activity that channelled kids' enthusiasm toward learning

RIGHT TO PLAY'S RED BALL

Right To Play's symbol is a red ball inscribed with the words "Look After Yourself, Look After One Another" in different languages. These words represent the values held by so many athletes: respect, cooperation, inclusion and fair play. RTP's red ball is not just a "mascot" that is pulled out at fundraising galas; it is RTP's teaching tool too, and every community that experiences RTP programming is given one of the red balls. Project coordinators and local coaches around the world use their red balls to empower people to look after themselves and their communities.

Ric Young, a social marketer from Toronto and one of RTP's advisors, came up with the idea for the red ball. Ric was thinking about a story his tailor had told him years earlier. His tailor was from a small village in southern Italy, where parents had little money for extras, even around Christmastime. One particular Christmas, the community of parents wanted to give something to their children, so they banded together and bought one ball, which they then gave to all the children in the village. "This story shows the genius of community," Ric says. And RTP adopted the idea, making a single ball a symbol of hope and the power to overcome hardship through cooperation, through teamwork.

THE MEDICAL TEAM

I had a medical team monitor my health from late 2009 up until the end of 2011. The team included Dr. Bill Hanlon, physician; Serge Tessier, physical therapy consultant; Andrea Lympany, nutritionist; Dr. Greg Long, chiropractor; Dr. Kelly Brett, specialist; and Lisa Benz, mental trainer. Every month, I went in for blood tests, checking hemoglobin, hematocrit and platelet count, as well as cholesterol, sodium and potassium levels. Periodically I had echo EKGs, VO_2 max tests and bone density analyses.

to work together, to find confidence in themselves, to become leaders. Injured or not, I knew I was even more determined than ever to raise the $250,000 I had committed to raise: enough money for programs for 5,000 kids.

And so, with the kids in mind, I decided I would continue to do my school visits and some walking laps. I rounded out February with trips to the Hamptons School in Calgary, and Mitford Middle School, where I was met with the same enthusiasm for sport that I had seen across Africa. These kids knew they had a lot in common with the kids being helped through Right To Play. Mitford students had already raised money for Right To Play in 2009. Both schools invited me back to run later in the year. And I planned to be fit for them!

As part of my rehab plan, I went to see Dr. Greg Long, a chiropractor at ProActive Health in Cochrane who performed some active release therapy on my shin. He also worked on some inflexibility issues in my left ankle, which may have contributed to my shin problem, putting pressure on the tibialis anterior muscle, especially when I climbed hills. He continued working with both parts of my leg well into the spring. After that first visit, I felt better, so I readied myself for what would become my "Walking Marathons."

March came in like a lion, if a slow-paced, slightly lame, shuffling one. I decided to walk the first marathon of the month and see how things held together. I used walking poles to take some of the pressure off the muscle around my shin, and I slipped on some new shoes, donated to me by *Impact Magazine*. I also switched routes from the hilly Cochrane Foothills Marathon to the Cochrane West Point Marathon course, which follows the Bow River and is relatively flat. I ended that first day of March with a time of 8:18:00, and my shin felt pretty good, even after a twinge at the 30 km mark.

During my half-month of walking marathons, I found that my cold-weather gear strategy didn't work as well for me as when I was running the marathons in sub-zero temperatures. I just couldn't

ATHLETE AMBASSADOR FOR RIGHT TO PLAY: WAYNE GRETZKY

In the early 1980s I was lucky enough to get tickets to see the Edmonton Oilers and watch probably the greatest player ever to put the "biscuit between the pipes." Time moves on, and it was with a measure of pride that on February 13, 2010, in between marathons, I watched Wayne Gretzky carry the Olympic torch on its route through the city of Vancouver. It was raining and Wayne was in the back of a pickup truck. It's hardly surprising that he is an athlete ambassador for Right To Play. Seems like all my sports heroes are!

THE WALKING MARATHONER'S PLAYLIST

During the month of March, when I was reduced to walking my marathons, I started compiling a playlist of "walking" songs with the help of members of the Marathon Quest 250 online community. By the end of the year, we had put together a great list. If you ever find yourself needing inspirational walking songs, try these out:

"I'm Gonna Be (500 Miles)," The Proclaimers
"These Boots Are Made for Walking," Nancy Sinatra
"Walk Like an Egyptian," The Bangles
"Walk Like You Don't Mind," Blue Rodeo
"Walk of Life," Dire Straits
"Walk on By," Susan Ashton
"Walk on the Wild Side," Lou Reed
"Walk On," Kellie Coffey
"Walk Tall," Val Doonican
"(I) Walk the Line," Johnny Cash
"Walkin' Blues," Eric Clapton
"Walking in the Rain," Walker Brothers
"Walking on Sunshine," Katrina and the Waves
"Walking on the Moon," The Police
"Walking on Thin Ice," Yoko Ono

seem to warm up. But, I persevered. I knew my muscle would recuperate eventually, that I wouldn't have to walk forever. I walked around the Cochrane course, and I also walked at a variety of schools and along some Calgary pathways.

I didn't really try running again until March 12, when I revisited the Marion Carson School, this time to pick up a cheque for $1,182.70. The previous day I had run a little bit during my walking marathon at Elboya School in Calgary, so after thanking the kids at Marion Carson, I headed out onto the Calgary pathways system and completed my marathon, doing five minutes of walking followed by five minutes of running, the whole way. It worked! In the meantime, I continued with the physio and active release therapy. I was definitely gaining strength.

By March 24, Marathon 049, I was back running again, which was good, because otherwise I may not have been able to follow the running tips I received that day from Jonathan, in Grade 2 at Belfast Elementary School in Calgary. While running circuits around a 480 m field, the kids came out for recess and Jonathan joined me to show me his new running technique. Did you know that if you keep your hands straight and pump your arms you can run like a ninja? I tried it for a lap or two. It was −11°c that day and running like a ninja helped keep me warm, as did the 220 kids who joined me at intervals throughout the marathon.

Spring felt closer when I did the Friendship Run in the town of Okotoks, Alberta, on March 27. The actual run was 23 km, but for me it would be Marathon 050. I had to wake up extra early to make it to Okotoks and start at 6:00 to make up the extra 19 km. It was a beautiful morning, no wind and 0°c. A few other runners started with me before being joined by even more people, including Sue, at around 8:45 a.m. for the Friendship Run. As we ran along the pathways by the hay fields, the sun's rays caught the mountaintops of the front ranges west of the town. One of the runners, Alan, was an ultrarunner, and after chowing down on some amazing chocolate chip cookies at an aid station, we chatted about ultras like "the toughest footrace in the world": Badwater in Death Valley, California; the Comrades in South Africa; and running the Grand Canyon rim to rim to rim. It was a great day, a gateway into the next of the four seasons of my quest, and, to top it all off, the Okotoks Running Club raised $920 that day for RTP and the kids!

DEVELOPING SELF-CONFIDENCE THE RTP WAY: LITERACY LADDER

During the winter season of Marathon Quest 250, I had some moments where I needed to boost my self-confidence in order to get out there and run, despite my injury. RTP recognizes that self-confidence is an essential skill for kids who are learning to be community advocates. The game Literacy Ladder makes learning the alphabet fun and helps build literacy and concentration, which increases self-confidence in participants.

To play Literacy Ladder, kids divide into two teams and sit facing one another so that their feet touch, forming two lines. The coach gives every kid an alphabet letter, the same one to each pair of kids facing each other. When the coach calls out a letter, the two children assigned with that letter get up, hop over the legs of the children before them (like climbing a ladder), run around to the beginning of the line, and then hop into their original spots on the line. Each kid has a few chances to climb the ladder.

After the game the coach asks the kids to think about why it's important to know the alphabet. By connecting the game to daily life, the kids begin to identify, sound out and put words together – a first step toward reading and self-confidence.

WINTER STATS

BEST QUESTION ASKED BY A CHILD: "Who is your favourite friend?"
PRODUCT OF THE SEASON: Hand Warmers
NUMBER OF MARATHONS: 53
NUMBER OF MARATHON RACES: 0
DISTANCE COVERED: 2,236.6 km
STEPS TAKEN: 2,738,646
SHOES USED: 5 pairs
EQUIVALENT FLIGHT DISTANCE: Calgary to Carlsbad, New Mexico
NUMBER OF SCHOOLS / DAY CAMPS VISITED: 10
AMOUNT OF MONEY RAISED FOR RTP: $19,286.02
NUMBER OF CHILDREN WHO RAN WITH ME: 1,997
AVATAR "MARATHON MARTIN": Red Rock, Northern Ontario

9

SPRING: NOT WITH A BANG, BUT A WHIMPER

"You have to forget your last marathon before you try another. Your mind can't know what's coming."

—FRANK SHORTER, runner

Ah, April showers. Spring cheered my spirits. Right To Play had been following my progress and providing support whenever needed; Robert and Beckie were always available if I had any questions. I seemed to have conquered my shin problem, and I was mixing up my routes a bit, both in Cochrane and in Calgary. I had also booked myself into some marathon races during the spring months, and these would break up my days. Somehow I had found a groove in this new, extreme lifestyle I was leading. Now, if only I could have accounted for the wind, I would have been on easy street.

By April 1 I'd finally established a good marathon route in Cochrane: west on Highway 1A for 13 km toward Ghost Lake and Ghost Station for a snack, then on for a couple more kilometres before turning around and heading home. I usually arrived home with 30 km in the bag before taking a quick break and running the remaining 12.2 kilometres along the river pathways. The only problem with the route was wind. If it was at my back when I began, I knew it would be a long day. Starting out with a headwind meant I would run into the wind during the first two and a half hours before turning around and being blown home.

It was on one of my first runs on this course that I came across an item I would keep in my running pack for the rest of the year. It was an Imperial Storm Trooper action figure, which I found in the

AVATAR "MARATHON MARTIN"

By April 6, Marathon 057, Avatar "Marathon Martin" had made good time along the north shore of Lake Superior on his virtual route across Canada.

Avatar "Marathon Martin" arrives at White River, Ontario, home of Winnie the Pooh.

THE 5MAW DIET PLAN

In January 2010 I had run 28 marathons and lost 2.7 kg. Could my routine be the answer the $40-billion diet industry has been looking for? The five-marathons-a-week (5MAW) diet plan! Eat whatever you want and you'll lose 8.2 kg in three months or your money back! Of course, my struggle was not to lose weight but to maintain it. I needed to keep my weight constant at 77 kg, and by early February I realized I needed a diet plan that would make up for the 5,000 calories I was burning five days a week. My nutritionist, Andrea, was recommending the full-fat diet: 3 per cent yogourt, cheese, full sour cream, 3 per cent milk, and ice cream. Andrea's diet worked pretty well. Over the course of the year I dropped 3.1 kg, but I felt good.

gravel by the curb at Ghost Station. I couldn't leave him there, so I picked him up. We were now a team!

The mornings became brighter and brighter, with fewer sub-zero days plaguing my runs. However, I did encounter a few obstacles in the spring: wind, snow, rain and, on the Calgary pathways, aggressive geese and their excrement. I was still working through my shin issues, but with continued physio I was able to keep running. I did have a couple of other injuries and health issues that season to add to my troubles: first a pinched nerve in my back that not even "extra-strength" Advil could cure and due to which I unfortunately had to cancel a run at Sam Livingstone School. Then, later in the season, I pulled a muscle in my leg. Neither injury put me completely out of commission, though.

As I increased my calorie intake and ran along my new marathon course, I buoyed myself up with thoughts of my running idols: Alf Tupper, Cliff Young, Sister Madonna Buder and others. I also reflected on what for me and many Canadians was a pretty significant anniversary. On April 12, 1980, Terry Fox dipped his foot in St. John's harbour and began his Marathon of Hope to raise money for cancer research. Terry was a Canadian humanitarian, athlete and cancer research activist. Though the spread of his cancer forced him to end his quest after 143 days and 5,280 km, and ultimately cost him his life, his determination and example created a lasting legacy. Terry ended up raising $22-million during his run from St. John's to Thunder Bay, Ontario. The foundation that bears his name has raised nearly half a billion for cancer research.

Thirty years after Terry started his marathon, I headed out on my Cochrane–Ghost Station run. I thought about what I was trying to do and hoped I could sustain the effort. To seal my pact with myself, I finished that day's work with what was becoming my customary single-scoop chocolate-fudge-chunk in a chocolate waffle cone at MacKay's, Cochrane's world-class ice creamery. I was the only one at the ice-cream counter ... maybe the weather had something to do with it!

THE RUNNING PLAYLIST

I was back at a run in the spring! My online supporters helped me create this fine playlist of running songs:

"Band on the Run," Wings
"Born to Run," Bruce Springsteen
"I Run for Life," Melissa Etheridge
"I'm Gonna Run Away," Bronski Beat
"Keep on Running," Steve Winwood
"Keep on Running," Stevie Wonder
"Long May You Run," Neil Young
"One Last Run," Nickelback
"Rabbit Run," Eminem
"Ready to Run," Dixie Chicks
"Run Run," Slade
"Run to Him," Bobby Vee
"Run to the Hills," Iron Maiden
"Run to You," Brian Adams
"Run with the Wolves," The Prodigy
"Run, Run, Run," Joel Plaskett
"Run," Snow Patrol
"Runaround Sue," Dion and the Belmonts
"Runaway," Run DMC
"Runaway," The Corrs
"Running on Empty," Jackson Brown
"Running on Faith," Eric Clapton
"Running Scared," Roy Orbison
"Running up that Hill," Kate Bush
"Running with the Devil," Van Halen
"Running," Jully Black
"The Runner," Manfred Mann
"Where Are We Running?" Lenny Kravitz

During the previous seven years that comprised my running life, April, and the spring and summer months that follow, had been destination months, the months in which I ran triathlons, marathons and ultras. This year would be no different, even though I'd basically been involved in a continuous ultra since the beginning of January. In the spring, I would run four official marathons: Boston, Vancouver, Red Deer and Calgary. First up, Boston.

One race team I had become aware of over the past few years would also be competing in Boston in 2010. This team demonstrates the true meaning of the human spirit. Team Hoyt is father Dick and son Rick from Massachusetts. They compete together in marathons, triathlons and other athletic endeavours. Rick has cerebral palsy caused by loss of oxygen to his brain at birth. Ignoring the advice that Rick should be put in an institution, Dick and his wife Judy supported their son's educational and athletic aspirations throughout his growing years, often having to forge new trails and fight for Rick's right to learn, to play. Dick and Rick started racing together when Rick wanted to take part in a 5-mile race to benefit a lacrosse player who had become paralyzed in an accident. Once begun, they continued to compete together. During a swim event, Dick pulls Rick in a special boat. In a bike event, Rick sits in a special seat fixed to the front of Dick's bike, and on the run is pushed in a special wheelchair. Through the Hoyt Foundation, the pair raise money to support people living with disabilities. I really wanted to meet this father–son team, and I tried to work out what I would say to them when I did.

My first marathon in Boston that year was not the official one. On April 18 I arose and completed a route up Columbus Street to the Boston Commons and then five loops of the Freedom Trail before finishing up at the John Hancock Sports & Fitness Expo, where I picked up my race package for the next day and had a look around. I noticed Rick and Dick at the expo and stopped in at the Team Hoyt table. I was delighted to have the opportunity to meet them and wished them all the best the next day before heading back to my hotel.

The last time I had run the Boston Marathon, in 2008, Boston Common was chaotic before the race, and as a result I almost missed my start time! This time, though, things went smoothly and I arrived in Hopkinton in plenty of time. My friends Cathy, Wayne and Michelle headed to their corrals and I to mine. I was supposed to be in corral #9 but decided to drop back to #13, the last one in the first wave. There was a half-hour gap between waves one and two, so I pretty much had the road to myself for about an hour before I heard the thunder of racing feet and thousands of runners poured past me.

I had planned a run–walk, 5:30:00 marathon, but I must admit I was caught up in the excitement: my half-marathon split was 2:15:00 even. The spectators were going wild and at one point it felt like I was participating in the Tour de France, with people converging on both sides and hundreds of high-fives being offered. The final 200 m was amazing, and I was thrilled with my time of 4:42:41.

Whenever I travelled to official marathons, I tried to make up for my travel days either by taking a day from the bank, or by running an extra day that week. I found I needed to take a banked day after Boston: the long downhills had pummelled my quads, and my first day out back home found my legs a little fragile. But by the time I headed to Westbrook School, north of Cochrane, I was feeling better.

I was always a bit nervous about what the schools would have in store for me in terms of a route. In the winter, I sometimes had to run back and forth numerous times along a cleared path in front of a school. Other times, a lovely loop would be marked out for me around a playground. At Westbrook the distance around the soccer fields was 500 m, which was perfect: 84 loops and I would be done!

Throughout the year, when I ran at schools, people asked me, "Don't you get bored running around in circles?" I must be a

SPRINGTIME RUNNING IN ALBERTA: MARATHON 072, APRIL 28, 2010

I had to get my car serviced at the Mazda dealership 25 km east of Cochrane. It was raining a bit, so I put on my light running tights and a jacket, dropped the car off and started to run loops around the dealership lot. The rain turned to sleet, then snow. Luckily, I had my emergency rain jacket: a Glad garbage bag with holes for the head and arms. My feet got wet and my woollen gloves quickly became sodden. Growing concerned, I stopped in to see how long the car would be and was told they would need another hour. I toughed it out for another 20 minutes, managing to cover 17 km and then went in to wait.

I drove home and threw all the clothes in the dryer. Then I upgraded my runners to trail shoes, switched to winter tights, grabbed a Stormtech jacket and put on some mitts. I headed down to see Amy at the Boys & Girls Club. By the time I got there my tights and feet were soaked, Amy gave me a cup of tea and told me they had collected $230 from the participants of a race they had organized. I thanked her and ran back along the river path to the house. When I got home I threw all the clothes in the dryer.

It was time to get serious. I upgraded my trail shoes to a pair of Salomon XT wings Gore-Tex and put on a pair of Stormtech pants. I was ready for anything. I decided not to go too far from the house, so I did loops around a new development nearby. Things went well for a while, but eventually water found a way in. I finished the marathon and trudged home. Again I threw all the clothes in the dryer.

glass-half-full kind of guy. The loops meant I wouldn't have to battle the wind all the time, and as the days got warmer and warmer I even got a nice tan on my legs (much like a rotisserie chicken). Also, how could I be bored running at a school when I got to run with so many different kids? Some came out, dashed ahead and then went to play soccer. Others ran with me for a while, then had a sore leg, stomach, arm, head [insert body part here] and called it quits. But, there were always one or two kids who got it and stuck with me for long stretches. You'd think it would have been the older kids who felt compelled to stay with me, but throughout the year I found Grade 1s and 2s seemed to stick like glue. At Westbrook my hero was 7-year-old Jade "The Machine." She came out four times that day and ran 19 loops (9.5 km). She was going to run 20 loops, but her teacher called her in for class.

From the perfect loops, perfect running partner and perfect weather at Westbrook, things took a turn for the worse when April ended with a snow day during which I slowly carved my way through blowing snow, alone. Ah, Alberta in the spring. Of course, the award going out to worst springtime running conditions is a toss-up for me between spring snow days – heavy, wet snow that sneaks into all gear regardless of technology – and spring "goose" days.

I always seem to encounter geese along the Elbow River pathway, by the Calgary Stampede Grounds. By the beginning of May, almost all the ice was gone and the birds were flocking in, including the noble Canada goose. The geese were everywhere, hissing and looking mean. As well, they contributed to the condition of the pathways with their incessant pooping: that stuff is slick. I almost fell headfirst on the pathway one morning because of the stuff, and the attack-mode that seems to be the default attitude for our national bird made me wonder if I should start carrying my running poles just to keep them at bay.

May began with the BMO Vancouver Marathon, one of Canada's largest, which has been run since 1972, when Tom Howard of

WHEN LIFE HANDS YOU LEMONS ...

After I almost took a fall slipping on goose poop, I remembered an old saying: "When life hands you lemons, make lemonade." I started to think that surely there was an application for a product as slippery as this stuff. The answer was obvious: I needed to find a way to market it to the Olympic bobsled team. If the goose product were applied to the runners of the sled, what chance would other teams have? I knew, however, that I would have to check the IOC's book on banned substances before I became too excited. Alas, they didn't seem to cover it.

THE BIGGEST SQUARE

When I introduced the Rice Krispie square fundraising idea to my loyal blog readers, Abbi, aged seven, asked me, "What was the biggest Rice Krispie square ever made?" Turns out our neighbours to the south at Iowa State University, on April 19, 2001, set the record for largest Rice Krispie square. Over 100 staff and students in Friley Hall kitchen took part in the eight-hour endeavour, using 818 lb. of Rice Krispies, 1,466 lb. of marshmallows and 217 lb. of butter to make the beast. It was then loaded on a truck and weighed. The 12 ft. long, 6 ft. wide and 2 ft. deep Rice Krispie square – in this case, rectangle – weighed in at a delicious 2,480 lb. After the official weighing, it was cut up and sold, with the proceeds going to charity.

Surrey, BC, led a small pack of runners around five loops of Stanley Park. Howard won the race with a time of 2:24:08, and he won again the following two years. Back then the race was called the British Columbia Marathon, and it's gone through some different titles since, but it remains a great marathon with a beautiful course. These days, the route runs along the other side of Burrard Inlet, along Marine Drive near the University of British Columbia and into Pacific Spirit Park.

When I returned to Alberta, I ran an extra day to make up for my travel time west and back. By May 6 I was back in Calgary, this time at Ranchlands School, where I met some kids who had figured out a great way to fundraise for Marathon Quest 250. As I completed my 52 loops around an 800 m course, I asked Grade 5 student Scott how the school had raised the $330 they had given me. Turns out the good ol' Rice Krispie square was their means to that lucrative end: at $1 per square, the kids were able to raise that much over two days. Thus began the great Rice Krispie Square Fundraiser, and questions from kids far and wide about this most North American of desserts poured in to my blog. I became so enmeshed in the lore of Rice Krispie squares that I started to think Vancouver should consider handing them out at their aid stations!

Thoroughly sticky with research on the almighty square, I went in for my regular visit to Dr. Greg at ProActive Health. It was the usual active release session on my shin, ankle and calf, but I also brought another concern to the table. I was starting to wonder if what I had thought was a pinched nerve earlier in the spring had been the start of something bad. Over the past couple of weeks, I'd been having some tightness and pain in my lower back. Dr. Greg checked it out and told me that my right side was a mess. (Of course, I wasn't terribly deterred, because in previous sessions he had found problems with my right quads, calf and ankle.) He warmed up my back and then gently worked some of the muscles. Then the real business began. He called in his assistant, Sara, and together they bent me into a pretzel. They pushed my right knee up around my ear, and then the evil Dr. Greg started to work on a muscle in my gluteus maximus. It hurt. I cried like a baby. However, later, my back felt fantastic. As the song goes, "You gotta be cruel to be kind."

Anyone who had run as much as I had was bound to experience the vagaries of stress injuries. I'll admit that I worried a bit about what my "older" body would be capable of. It turned out I was doing better than many people had predicted, even Serge, at Cochrane Sport Physio. Shortly after seeing Dr. Greg, I went for a VO_2 max test at Serge's office. We wanted to see what had changed over the last four months. VO_2 max is the maximum capacity of an individual's body to transport and utilize oxygen during incremental exercise; it reflects the physical fitness of the individual tested, his or her endurance capability. When Serge gave me the results, he seemed pleased: "Your VO_2 max has increased from 50.3 to 53.3 ml/kg/min. To no surprise, this score places you in a category well above average, but what is surprising is that despite your long history as an endurance athlete, you continue to show measurable, significant increases in your peak VO_2. I anticipated seeing your profile change from the first to second, but I was surprised to see this increase."

I too was surprised and pleased with the result. As warmer temperatures were headed my way, I knew I would need all the fitness I could muster. I always have done better in cold temperatures, so I knew that the warm weather to come would be throwing some challenges my way. The day of my VO_2 max test, I ran 18 km of my marathon with Neil and the Cool Kids Running Club at Fish Creek Park in Calgary, and already I realized I needed to pull out my "Martin of Arabia" headgear, which protects my head (bald), ears (big), neck (red) and the top of my shoulders (white).

It was soon time for my third official marathon of the season, Marathon 089 in Red Deer. By this point I had run 3755.8 km in

Sue at the Right To Play booth at the Red Deer marathon expo.

ANNIE'S GIFT = A CLASSROOM'S YEAR-LONG RTP EXPERIENCE

I ran Marathon 082 with my friend Annie, who graciously sponsored me for $1,000 to celebrate her birthday. This amount would allow a classroom of children to receive a Right To Play program for a year: 20 kids would receive a gift that could change their lives forever.

In 2010 Right To Play marked its 10th anniversary and asked its staff and volunteers, the kids in the programs, teachers and other partners to think about what RTP meant to them. They received a deluge of comments, one of which was from Musarrat, a 10-year-old girl from Pakistan, a polio survivor who had once spent most of her time alone but was drawn out and boosted up by a Right To Play coach in her community. She wrote: "I used to think I would never perform any other role apart from sitting in a wheelchair. Now I lead activities for more than 45 children in my school."

my quest. Although the race wasn't until Sunday, May 23, Sue and I headed up on the Friday and set up a Right To Play booth at the race expo. I had also been asked to be one of the guest speakers that day and the next. All my experience speaking in front of kids that year paid off! At the expo, I was lucky to meet Jack Cook, an ultra-marathoner who owns Fast Trax Run & Ski Shop in Edmonton. When he found out about the quest, he gave me two pairs of New Balance 1062s.

So it was with new shoes that I sprinted out of the dock on that chilly Sunday morning, along with 1,200 others, all bundled up for the race. The half- and full-marathon participants were all mixed together. I felt very good, so I went off like a bullet. I covered the first half in 2:07:00, dodging around people and flying along the trails. This was not the plan. I was meant to be steady, under control. I was in the midst of a year of marathons, and it wasn't like I was in top form – I was still dealing with my shin and my back tension. The trouble is, the first half of a race sometimes brings out the worst in me. I was thinking, "Hey, I feel great, so why not pick the pace up a bit? Maybe today will be a 4:10:00 or a 4:15:00!" It would not. My enthusiasm started to wane around the 28 km mark. I reasoned, "There's no rush," and "Don't get yourself injured," and "You've got another one tomorrow." I started to be sensible and slowed down. I came in at around 4:30:00, which was just fine by me.

Although I'm not at my best in hot temperatures, I prefer a bit of heat to a deluge any day. It seemed that whenever I checked the temperature at the end of May I saw forecasts like "rain show-ers with 100 per cent chance of precipitation." Not good. I spent a lot of time in my Glad-bag getup, running around muddy tracks at schools, slipping in wet goose poop on the trails. The one fun thing about the rain was borrowing cool umbrellas from the kids at Tuscany Elementary School in Calgary on May 27. On every walk break I would borrow an umbrella from one of the students, each representing a different theme. I walked beneath the shelter of the

BAREFOOT RUNNERS

As spring wore on, I started to see more and more articles about barefoot running. I read one piece after the Red Deer Marathon about a woman in Halifax who ran a 10 km race barefoot. She said that her feet didn't feel bad, but her ankles, knees, hips and back hurt. Although I never considered running the quest barefoot, when I started Marathon Quest 250, I thought it would be neat to run all 250 marathons in just three pairs of shoes. These were my old runners, and I didn't have a shoe sponsor. I think, however, that my Marathon 028 stress injury cropped up because of a few things – my inflexible ankle, a hilly course and worn-out runners. The time I took off at the beginning of that injury made me realize that I like shoes with support.

During the quest I didn't get a shoe manufacturer to sponsor me, so I relied on the generosity of friends and independent sport stores. By the middle of May, I had used nine pairs of shoes, eight different brands, and sustained three blisters. By the end of June, when I picked up three new pairs of shoes, one from Gord's Running Store and the others from the New Balance Store in Crowfoot, Calgary, I added another brand to the list: Mizuno.

Little Mermaid, a zebra, *Cars* (the movie), pink hearts, Beauty & the Beast, Cinderella, and Spiderman. I also collected soggy and slick donations, from a once-crisp $10 bill to some wet and shiny pennies found on the grass. At the end of that marathon I ran into the gym and all the teachers, volunteers and kids gave a huge cheer. During the day the kids had raised $2,105.37 with a collection at school, online donations, money given to me and pennies found on the playground. I didn't feel soggy when I left, but buoyant: I was coming closer and closer to my goal for RTP.

On June 6, *Impact Magazine* sponsored my hundredth marathon. I ran in downtown Calgary, joined part of the way by a group doing a walk for multiple sclerosis. Elaine Kupser and Pete Estabrooks from the magazine were there too. I met them at Eau Claire market, where I often enjoyed the coffee and muffins from the Good Earth Café. A few of my friends from the Cochrane club came out, as did other running friends I'd met through the course of the year. It was a seven-minute run/three-minute walk routine. We topped the marathon off with a fantastic carrot cake from the Good Earth, with "Congratulations on the 100th" written in cream-cheese icing on the top.

A fantastic article in the *Globe and Mail* launched me into the summer months. While the article's author, Hayley Mick, acknowledged some of the skepticism I had faced at the beginning of the quest in 2009–2010 – the quibbles of health professionals who believed I would exit the quest in rough shape – she also suggested I was in good health – and I did feel good! She noted that at this point I had run the distance from Cochrane to Rimouski, Quebec. It was great to hit the 100th marathon but I still had another 150 to go, and I still had a lot of fundraising to do.

I know Sue was feeling disappointed for me at how the fundraising was going by the 100th run. I had completed 40 per cent of the marathons but only raised $42,051.03, which was a mere 17 per cent of the $250,000 target. However, Sue always had great faith that I would complete the 250 marathons, and that would be a great achievement in itself. She was always saying how proud she was of me and of what I was trying to achieve. We agreed that any money raised was worthwhile, and even if only a few children would benefit, that was better than none at all. I know there were times when she worried about my fitness and felt like telling me to stop. But she didn't do that because what I really needed was for her to be positive and supportive.

BEST MARATHON SNACKS

- Single scoop, double chocolate with fudge chunks, chocolate waffle cone from MacKay's in Cochrane
- A slice of pizza during Pizza Days at the schools
- Snickers or Kit-Kat bar and coffee at Ghost Station
- Hickory Sticks from the Shouldice Pool vending machine.
- Coffee and muffin at Good Earth Cafe, Eau Claire Market, Calgary

AVATAR "MARATHON MARTIN" ARRIVES IN BOSTON

At precisely 2:54 p.m. on Sunday, June 6, Avatar "Marathon Martin" entered the Boston city limits. He had started his virtual route across Canada and the U.S. on January 1, at the intersection of the 1A Highway and Horse Creek Road, just outside Cochrane, Alberta. His virtual running route had taking him through the Canadian provinces of Alberta, Saskatchewan, Manitoba, Ontario and Quebec, at which point he entered the U.S. and travelled through Vermont, New Hampshire and into Massachusetts. Now, it was time to head west again.

Avatar "Marathon Martin" outside the Museum of Fine Art in Boston, Massachusetts.

June would be the marker for a few different things, the 100th marathon, the halfway point (at the end of the month) and, of course, the end of my school marathons, until September, that is. During the last week of June I ran three marathons at schools, starting off on the solstice at Mount View and finishing up at Elizabeth Barrett School in Cochrane, where I ran a 420 m loop 100 times and took some breaks to chat with kids about gophers. The school's field had loads of holes and the kids said the rodents were a menace; they were ruining their play field. I suggested that the school create a gopher town with little houses for them. The kids were not impressed and said they should all be killed. Ruthless little darlings.

The hard-core attitude at Elizabeth Barrett extended to some of the runners who joined me, one of whom, Grade 2 student Gabby, shared a poem with me. She told me she always repeated the following mantra in her head when she ran:

Running's not work.
Don't be a squishy jerk.
Running is fun,
So run, run, run.

It worked for me then and still does today.

By the end of June I had reached the midpoint of the year, having run 119 marathons and 5000 km. I knew I would have to pick up the pace a bit; I had to complete 131 more in the second half. A number of kids asked me to give them a visual for what 5000 km represents, so I came up with some different road-trip scenarios:
- Canada: Vancouver, BC, to Chicoutimi, Québec
- USA: Bangor, Maine, to Barstow, California
- Europe: Lisbon, Portugal, to Sivas, Turkey
- Australia: Cairns, Queenland, to Busselton, Western Australia
- Africa: Cape Town, South Africa, to Zanzibar, Tanzania

ATHLETE AMBASSADOR FOR RIGHT TO PLAY: KYLE SHEWFELT

I met Kyle Shewfelt in June 2010 at the Red Ball RTP golf tournament in Canmore and have stayed in contact with him ever since. He is a Canadian gymnast who won gold in the men's floor exercise competition at the 2004 Athens Olympics. His was the first medal ever won by a Canadian in an artistic gymnastics event. He continues to associate himself with the Olympics and worked as CTV's gymnastics analyst for the 2012 summer Olympics in London. He is also an athlete ambassador for Right To Play, helping the organization raise money and spreading the word about RTP's amazing programs. Kyle visited Liberia in 2011 and joined in with RTP programming there. He has also inspired many to donate to RTP, including a young gymnast named Elijah, who met Kyle in 2007 and kept in touch with him. Elijah surprised Kyle in 2011 when he sent him $100 for RTP, money Elijah had saved up by getting his parents to sponsor him: $1 for every new skill he learned in gymnastics. Now, that's putting sport to good use!

END OF SEASON STATS TO DATE

BEST QUESTION ASKED BY A CHILD: "How do you like being a boy?"
PRODUCT OF THE SEASON: Glad 3-in-1 Rain Jacket
NUMBER OF MARATHONS: 119
NUMBER OF MARATHON RACES: 4
DISTANCE COVERED: 5,021.8 km
NUMBER OF STEPS TAKEN: 6,089,892
NUMBER OF SHOES USED: 12 pairs
EQUIVALENT FLIGHT DISTANCE: Calgary to Honolulu, USA
NUMBER OF SCHOOLS / DAY CAMPS VISITED: 24
AMOUNT OF MONEY RAISED FOR RTP: $46,546.35
NUMBER OF CHILDREN WHO RAN WITH ME: 4,824
AVATAR "MARATHON MARTIN": Rochester, New York

10
SUMMER: HIGHS AND LOWS

"Why couldn't Pheidippides have died at mile 20?"
                                    −slogan on a T-shirt

I had some hard times in the short summer season of 2010, when injuries seemed to plague my steps. But I had enough incentive to keep going: my family supported me, as did RTP and my local community. Of course, the lemonade and ice cream also helped …

I sometimes wondered about Tony Harris's initial question when he interviewed me on CNN in December 2009: "Are you nuts?" Was I crazy to do this 250-marathons-in-a-year quest, even if it was for a charity I believed in?

I decided to ask a disinterested outsider about the state of my mental health when I ran my first marathon of July in Calgary. I started out at Shouldice Pool at 8:30 a.m. and moved along through perfect running weather – cloudy, 15°c – to Good Earth and my muffin and coffee. Along the way, I met Florin, who had been following my blog. Florin was Romanian and a teacher at Chaparral School, but he also had a degree in psychology. I took the opportunity to ask him if he thought I was nuts. He said that by the strict medical definition, I wasn't. Good news. Then I asked him if I was addicted or had an obsession with running. He said I could only be called obsessed if running had an "overwhelming impact on my life." Hm.

During the summer holiday months I switched from school runs to summer day-camp runs so I could continue to run with kids. The first of these happened to fall on another quest marker, the halfway point: Marathon 125. I had run 5275 km, visited 24 schools and run with over 4,800 kids. However, I had only raised

TESTIMONIAL FROM TWIZERIMANA (AGE 14), RUBAVU DISTRICT, RWANDA

In 2010 Twizerimana from Rwanda sent Right To Play the following words to tell them how much their programs meant to her:

> I come from a very poor family. My mother is a single parent working hard to make ends meet. I used to be among the best pupils in class. But in Primary Grade 4, my grades dropped. My mother thought it was not necessary for me to continue to go to school, but I have always wanted to do well, dreaming of the day I would have a job and support my mother and family. Then, one day, our teacher took us to the playground and taught us a game called "A Blind Person Running with a Partner." This game taught us to recognize our weaknesses and respect our differences. I understood then that to achieve my goal I needed a partner. I decided to ask for support from Issa, the boy who always came first in our class.
>
> Issa started coaching me for one hour every day after school. As a result, by the end of the year, my grades were up again and I was ninth in the class. Amazed, my mother wanted to know how this happened. I explained that a Right To Play game taught me to detect and acknowledge my weakness and to seek support, which I did. Today Issa is my best friend and is always welcome to our home.

TERRY

On July 12th, at the YMCA day camp in Calgary, a boy asked me who my hero was, and I said, "Terry Fox." His was an appropriate question for me at this time in the quest. Terry had run 5,373 km from St. John's to Thunder Bay before he had to stop. That distance took him 143 days to complete; the same distance had taken me 193 days.

$51,722.77. I was disappointed to see I had reached halfway in distance but not in funds raised. I needed to raise a further $198,277.23 to keep my commitment to the 5,000 kids to whom I'd promised RTP programming.

If springtime weather in Alberta resembles a yo-yo in the hand of a child, summertime weather sometimes feels like a yo-yo in the hand of a competing yo-yo champion. There are just that many more extremes to exploit in the summertime, from intense dry heat to sub-zero temperatures, rain and sleet to thunderstorms and hail. I would get my share of all of them, as well as some mild, perfect running days. One afternoon, I ran near the Inglewood Bird Sanctuary in Calgary shivering in the cold and ducking hailstones. The very next day, I was running in 22°c, looking up at sunny skies.

As the days warmed up, Sue took to accompanying me more and more on my runs. She would join me for the morning, doing as much as a half-marathon, often 10 km tempo runs. When she registered for her first marathon – the Queen City Marathon in Regina on September 12 – she started doing long runs, up to 32 km, with me. After one of these long-run mornings in Cochrane, as I finished off my kilometres for the day, I ran right into a sight for sore eyes: a lemonade stand. I had no change on me, but the proprietors, Kyle and Joe, suggested that I "have a free one." These two 10-year-olds had an enterprise worth writing about. Lemonade Stand Inc. was no one-trick pony: Kyle and Joe supplied iced tea and cookies, and they planned to expand into snow cones. These guys were astute businessmen and agreed to my proposal: if they would supply me with lemonade when I saw them, I would promote their business on my website.

In addition to having the best lemonade this side of Edmonton at my disposal, I continued to keep my calorie count high by stopping in at MacKay's for ice cream. Now that ice cream weather was at hand, though, I began the daring task of trying all 47 flavours, from Alberta saskatoon berry to white chocolate raspberry truffle.

Above: Kyle and Joe's lemonade stand by the Bow River along the Cochrane pathways. Below: Another day, another fall. Must try and stay on my feet.

In the latter part of July, the sweet lemonade and ice cream helped me keep my mind off some of my aches and pains. This is when I was at my lowest point. I fell on the trail two days in a row, injuring my knees, and I was battling some shoulder and upper-thigh pain that Serge and Dr. Greg had trouble resolving. But even ice cream didn't make it all better. With something of a broken heart, I decided not to run in the San Francisco Marathon on July 26 as I'd planned.

Sue was a bit shocked. We had planned to do the first half together, so now she would be racing on her own, for the first time. I reasoned that taking a rest day would give me the opportunity to be support crew for Sue. Usually, she is my crew, supporting me at ultras and marathons. So, on July 26 I took my seat in the spectator shuttle and followed her, cheering and yelling my throat hoarse, around the beautiful, albeit hilly, course. She came in at around 2:30:00, an excellent time. She was delighted, not only to have run across the Golden Gate Bridge but also to be the proud wearer of one medal I didn't have! I have to say it is a good experience for a crazed runner like me to sit back and support another runner for a change.

My various injuries pointed me toward walking marathons again. They also led me to the realization, on July 27, that I had reached a critical juncture in MO 250. Plan A, to run 250 marathons in 2010 and use 12 spare days to recover from injuries, was torpedoed and had sunk. Of course, the plan had already taken a major hit in February when my shin injury required me to take 11 of the recovery days. Then I had to take my final spare day before the San Francisco Marathon. I reckoned I had to switch to Plan B – not a great plan but all I had. I continued to schedule myself to run five marathons a week and take two recovery days, but now I had to use those weekly recovery days should I sustain an injury. The San Francisco Marathon day turned out to be one of my weekly recovery days. Of course, there was also a Plan C, but it was horrible. This plan would kick in when I'd used all my recovery days and would then have to run every day. Not good. Plan D was simple: stay in bed.

My thigh seemed to hold up over the course of the first four-day stint of walking marathons, which represented what felt like a week of early mornings and long days, sometimes fighting mosquitoes and sunburn, invariably through hot temperatures. I felt a bit like Lawrence of Arabia, battling the vagaries of weather, trudging through the imaginary sands of southern Alberta. Kind of.

By August 4, the day I'd been invited to the Cochrane Day Camp to be a celebrity judge of the cinnamon-bun baking competition, I was still walking. A guy I met on the path asked me how everything was going, and I mentioned that I was walking my marathons lately because of an injury. He replied, "It must feel like a day off!" I felt like saying, "No, walking a marathon is not a day off. Contrary to popular belief, a walked marathon is the same distance as one taken at a run." My spirits perked up, however, when some of the kids at the day camp joined me on my route and one little girl asked, "Where are we going?" I said, "Nowhere!" Of course, I was feeling great by the time I had to play Simon Cowell at the cinnamon-bun bake-off. All the baking groups somehow received the same number of points, though in different categories: presentation, creativity, flavour integration and taste. Yum.

In mid-August Sue and I flew to Ontario. Our daughter Kristina was getting married, and I had three marathons to complete. I went to my old stomping grounds in Sudbury and ran a marathon through the rain with 16 old pals, including Vince and Stephanie. It was great to run on the Laurentian University track, and even better when my granddaughter, Autumn, aged six, joined me for four laps. Best yet: she beat me. I also completed a family walking marathon with my son, Kyle, in Sault Ste. Marie on August 13. We walked a 7.5 km loop along the waterfront and around Whitefish Island. The kids had shown me great support over the last several years and it was a thrill having them be part of Marathon Quest 250.

It was a wet week and a half and my trusty Glad 3-in-1 "rain jacket" came in handy as the weather alternated between downpour and sunlight. By the end of August I had used seven Glad jackets and the price of those babies is hard to beat.

Next stop was Toronto. I persisted in walking until August 24, Marathon 154, which I conducted as a walk–run in downtown Toronto with Right To Play president, CEO and founder Johann Olav Koss and 26 other RTP employees and some friends. Johann joined us at 8:30 a.m. as we started the marathon. He went into the lead and stayed there for most of the 10 km he completed with us. I could see that some of the old Olympic competitive spirit was still alive and well. David from the Tour d'Afrique joined us as well. It was great to see him, so many races later! We ended the marathon at the Winston Churchill statue in Nathan Phillips Square, which I thought was appropriate. Churchill did once say, "It is not enough that we do our best; sometimes we have to do what is required."

END OF SEASON STATS TO DATE

BEST QUESTION ASKED BY A CHILD: "Where are we going?"
PRODUCT OF THE SEASON: MacKay's Ice Cream
NUMBER OF MARATHONS: 159
NUMBER OF MARATHON RACES: 4
DISTANCE COVERED: 6,709.8 km
NUMBER OF STEPS TAKEN: 8,213,876
NUMBER OF SHOES USED: 16 pairs
EQUIVALENT FLIGHT DISTANCE: Calgary to Liverpool, UK
NUMBER OF SCHOOLS / DAY CAMPS VISITED: 29
AMOUNT OF MONEY RAISED FOR RTP: $66,791.19
NUMBER OF CHILDREN WHO RAN WITH ME: 5,789
AVATAR "MARATHON MARTIN": Black River Falls, Wisconsin

By the time I returned to Alberta, the summer was coming to an end and I was looking forward to more school visits, back to the old routine. I have to say that I missed not doing a tri or an ultra or even an official marathon during the summer season. But that didn't stop me from dreaming about them. By this time I had been asked a few times to reveal the name of the "hardest, toughest race around." I've heard a number of claims, but I decided, in my spare time that summer, to search the world for the toughest race. I checked out Africa, Asia and Australia, but I think I found the most difficult race right next door in the ol' U.S. of A.

In coming to this conclusion, I used the criterion of percentage of participants finishing. For example, in the 2009 Kona Ironman, 1,777 started and 1,650 finished (93 per cent). In the 2010 Badwater 135-mile ultra, 80 started and 73 finished (91 per cent). But the "toughest race" award has to go to the Barkley, held at the Frozen Head Park in Tennessee in late March. It's a 100-mile ultra that has been going for 10 years. Seven hundred people have started this race, and only nine have finished (1.3 per cent). The Barkley's motto could be: "If you finish, you are a winner!"

In a way, that's how I was feeling at the end of August. But I was determined to be a winner!

11

AUTUMN:
OUT OF THE DARKNESS
AND INTO THE LIGHT

"Don't be afraid to give up the good to go for the great."
—ANONYMOUS

How could I get back on the marathon horse after such a tough August? I suppose I had to accept that I was sustaining some injuries that I would have to manage day to day and take each day as it came. It seemed that as soon as I realized this, I started experiencing better runs. Of course, it helped that my health practitioners were at my side and giving their all. Regina Marathon, here Sue and I come!

I had had a brutal August, both physically and mentally. I had taken a number of falls and had walked more marathons than I had run. Mentally this was grinding me down. I didn't think I could keep it up for another four months and 90 marathons. I had a number of chats with Lisa, my mental trainer, and she encouraged me during this tough time. My leg was still acting up a bit at the beginning of September. Ever since I fell on my right hip in August, there had been an ache or pain somewhere in the leg – the side of my knee, in the hamstrings or quad or glute. But on September 4, I went to see Dr. Greg, who gave me the once over, causing extreme pain during the session, and the next morning something felt different: there was no pain in my right leg.

Cheered, I headed out to Calgary, and because it was raining I decided to throw caution to the wind. I planned to run two minutes, then walk eight, and see how the leg held up. Despite the rain, the leg felt great, and I completed a very satisfactory marathon. My maxim of late, however, seemed to be two steps forward, one step back. The next day, as I was finishing up my marathon in Calgary, I came across some kids playing soccer, the ball came my way and I gave it a good kick. There was a twinge in my knee and that begged for Advil when I got home.

I was glad I was feeling better because Sue and I had planned to run our first marathon together in Regina. After not running the San Francisco Marathon, I was determined to ensure I was in top form for Regina's Queen City Marathon in September. Sue's birthday was on September 10 and our wedding anniversary was on the 11th. However, the marathon was on the 12th, so we put the wine on ice.

Looking back at Sue's running log, she started running regularly in 2006. Her only run previous to that was when she and I hit the river pathways in Cochrane for the Terry Fox Run in 2005 on the weekend we got married and we thought it would be a fun thing to do together. It took us quite a time cover the 10 km, as we were laughing and chatting with everyone along the way and it was more of a walk than a run.

It took a long time for Sue to consider herself a runner. To be honest, when she first decided to buy some proper running gear and "give it a go," she really struggled. When I met her, she was a regular swimmer, but her main sport was fencing, her weapon of choice being the foil. She loved to compete and was lucky to have some of the Great Britain Olympic team as training partners.

In Cochrane it just so happened that all the people we socialized with were runners and triathletes, so it was almost inevitable that Sue would get involved. She did a couple of short triathlons but never felt at ease on the bike, so she decided to concentrate more on running.

Over the next few years, Sue completed two 5 km runs and a 10 km race in 2006; a 5 km and 10 km in 2007; a 5 km, four 10 km and a half-marathon in 2008; and two 10 km and two half-marathons in 2009. She admits she probably wouldn't have considered doing a marathon, but, "When your husband gets up and runs one nearly every day, you feel obliged to at least try one!"

The morning of the Queen City Marathon was sunny and cool. I met Scott Russell from CBC Sports at the start line, and we had a chat before the pistol sounded and Sue and I headed out. All was well for the first 24 km, and we kept up an 8 km/h pace. At 31 km, however, the wheels came off. Sue's calves were seizing up, so we sat on a bench for 15 minutes. A "Rolling Aid" lady came by on a mountain bike and asked Sue if she wanted a ride. These people sweep up at the back of the race to make sure everyone is okay. This offer seemed to galvanize Sue: there was no way she was going to get on the back of the bike. We started walking and then, to my surprise, Sue started running. We came in at just over 5:30:00. Not many people can say they celebrated their 58th birthday by running their first marathon. I was so proud of her!

When we returned from Saskatchewan, I went to see Dr. Hanlon in Cochrane. Although my leg was feeling a bit better since my session with Dr. Greg earlier in the month, I felt I needed some more feedback. First, Hanlon reviewed my blood work for the last two months, and everything looked good. I then told him about the pains in my right leg since I had the fall in August. He diagnosed that I had a muscle tear deep in my glute. This would be causing the pain in my right leg but not the pains in the knee. He commented that with the activity level I had planned to the end of the year, it would not heal. At the same time, he figured there was a good chance it wouldn't get any worse as long as I managed it day to day. After my session with Dr. Hanlon, I did a marathon in Calgary, then headed over to Dr. Greg, who worked the muscles in my back and right leg. He also ordered an x-ray to check out the injured hip.

In the meantime, it was business as usual. School was back in session, and I was back at school with the kids. It was also time for southern Alberta's autumn rainy season. On September 16, with rain gear on, I headed to St. Timothy School in Cochrane and ran with phys-ed teacher Travis and his cross-country team. I soon realized I was out of practice hurtling down trails and over rocks and tree roots. After 2 km with those extremists, I said goodbye. They were about to start a set of fartleks and that was not for me! Instead, I established a 600 m loop, and it took me most of the morning, walking–running, to complete 18 km.

I took a brief break to address the kids at 11:00, and someone in the audience asked, "Who is your competition?" It felt like an existential question to me when I was back outside in the rain, paying the price for the run with the cross-country team. The glute muscle started to ache, and I decided to walk the rest of the way. The marathon took so long to complete that the kids had finished school and were heading home when I still had 2 km left to go. Not a great day.

It would seem that my hopes were too high for the failing glute! When fall slipped into winter the next day, with a 0°c temperature that felt much colder, I decided to try one of my old spring routes along the 1A toward Ghost Station. I tried to run but the pain in the glute was back, and something was going on with my left leg. Ever since I had resolved the repetitive strain to the muscle in the left shin, the left leg had been performing at 100 per cent. I was very concerned when I started to feel something amiss at the top of that leg. I decided not to push things and walked the rest of the way. Sue joined me for the final 14 km. She had recovered well from the Queen City Marathon, and I was thankful for some company on the road.

I had to face the fact that, over the last month and a half, I had been in a rut. My right leg was a mess, my marathon times seemed to be getting slower and slower, and I was beginning to wonder where this was all leading. I couldn't bring myself to believe I was falling apart, though. Not now. I was so close! I had to keep it together and keep trying. My promise to Right To Play and all the kids I hoped to help really did keep me going. I think the shin injury in March had shown me I could work through an injury with the help of my physio team, Sue, and my own sensible actions, like walking my marathons instead of running them.

I was frustrated, but I knew I could work through the pain by being sensible, taking the good advice of my health-care providers, and that my body would slowly heal. I was determined.

My mood was brighter when I ran a United Communities marathon at Silverado in Calgary's southwest. I ran two such marathons that fall – the other at Sage Hill – both of which were wonderful events for Right To Play: United Communities donated $2,500 at each. Not only was the Silverado event good for the kids, it was also good for me. I started off slowly, expecting the pain in the right leg to return. But after 30 minutes I was still feeling good, so I pushed things along a little. Before I knew it, I had completed the marathon in 5:08:22. It was the fastest marathon I'd done since Marathon 108 on June 17. It was exactly the kind of confidence booster I needed – and to top everything off, I met some relatives of the incomparable, 99-years-young Fauja Singh, who I once cheered on at the Toronto Waterfront Marathon. I was reminded of my journey to this point in time, and of other runners who continue on, despite the odds.

My next few marathons were similarly uplifting. After one physio session, at which the therapist applied ultrasound to my left glute, I figured I would never walk again. But the next day, at Hawkwood School in Calgary, after a tentative start, the pain eased off after 3 km. Of course, getting to meet the kids and hear their incredible stories helped – one was about Pipsqueak the hamster, owned by Adam, who said that the small but mighty beast could run eight hours at a time on his treadmill. A Grade 2 girl told me I didn't look as young as I did on the Marathon Quest 250 poster. Who would after 173 marathons? But, I did feel younger than I had in a while.

September would be my month of physical and psychological

healing, I think. At the end of the month, Serge told me I was a tight ass, er, that my glute muscles were very tight and were pinching the sciatic nerve to the piriformis muscle. He had decided he would use acupuncture to relieve the nerve, and the results were excellent. I would go back for more acupuncture after that, and it helped enormously, as did a variety of stretches I started engaging in to prevent the glute from pinching the nerve. I felt I was finally on the road to recovery.

LEARNING PROBLEM-SOLVING SKILLS THE RTP WAY: HUMAN KNOT

Life is complicated and we need to solve many problems throughout the course of it. Right To Play coaches pull the Human Knot game out of their bag of tricks when they want to help kids understand how working together to problem-solve can lead to success.

To play the game, kids form a circle and face inward. Then, they move closer together and hold the hand or wrist of two other children across the circle from them. They must then cooperate to figure out how they are going to untangle themselves, without letting go of one another. They must step over and under arms, wiggle free and form a large open circle again, but still hold on. As they work, all of the kids are encouraged to take part in contributing ideas on how to get back to the open circle.

When the kids are finally at the end point, coaches ask them to reflect on how they worked as a team, and what qualities a strong leader needs to have. The coaches guide them as they speak about problem-solving, and how they might apply what they learned in Human Knot to other problems that might crop up in their lives.

As if to add a crown to September events, my marathon at Springbank Community High School was not only a great run, starting out with a glorious cross-country run with the school's running team and a great assembly with a Global Village theme, but after my talk about Right To Play and Marathon Quest 250, I was presented with an envelope and asked to open it. Inside was a cheque to Marathon Quest 250/Right To Play for $10,000. I was speechless, which is pretty unusual for me. Apparently, the kids had held a gala and an auction and had carried out extensive volunteer work to raise the funds. I am still amazed. Talk about teamwork!

Students from Springbank Community High School present me with a cheque to Right To Play for $10,000.

Dr. Hanlon and me outside Shouldice Pool at the start of marathon #183.

October started out with a bang when I ran with my friend and family doctor Bill Hanlon in Calgary. He had supported me from the start, so I was thrilled when he sponsored a marathon for $1,000. Of course, this little Calgary marathon we ran was nothing compared to some of Dr. Hanlon's accomplishments. He is:

- the founder and medical director of Basic Health International Foundation, based in Cochrane;
- a provider of health care to high-need, remote mountain communities in Ethiopia, Honduras, Peru, Mongolia and Tibet;
- a climber of Mount Everest in 2007, which was the last mountain he needed to climb to tick the seven continents' seven highest peaks off his mountain-climbing list; and
- an Antarctic ski trekker, having completed a 47-day odyssey to the South Pole in January 2010.

One of the schools I visited in October was the Hamptons, which I had first visited in March when I was injured. I was happy to be back there, this time in better form. Chico, the school's caretaker, had come out to join me when I ran my 100th marathon in June, and he was at the school to run with me that day in October, too. Chico and I ran with running club members and a couple of parents as well. I was really impressed with the number of running clubs I was seeing at the schools. Usually the kids in the clubs ran three days a week together, about a half-hour each time, counting their loops as they run around a track. At the Hamptons, when running club members hit 42 rounds of the track, they are awarded gold medals. Chico stuck with me throughout the marathon, and when we finished up at 2:00 the school presented us with cardboard "gold" medals along with a cheque for Right To Play.

I knew the gold medal I received at the Hamptons would be better than anything I'd get at the next official marathon I was tackling as part of Marathon Quest 250. My 188th marathon would be in Victoria on October 10. We left Calgary in blazing sunshine and arrived in Victoria in pouring rain, but we had hope that the next day's weather would be suitable for running. I ran with my friend Gerard; it was his first marathon!

I was feeling good, so Gerard and I at first tried a pace of 11 km/h. For the first hour, we were spot on, but then Gerard pulled ahead and I lost him. Still, I felt good about my pace, and my body felt fit. By two hours I was at 22 km and at the three-hour mark I was at 33.5 km. I made the decision to hammer home the final kilometres and came in at 3:43:43 (chip time). I was thrilled, pleased that I had run a "negative split," the holy grail for marathon runners. I ran the first 21.1 km in 1:53:58 and the second in 1:49:45. I later heard from Gerard, who had a great first half but then experienced bad cramps at the 24 km mark, which forced him to walk 8 km. He still finished in 4:21:0 and was ready to register for another race.

When I returned to Alberta from the island, I could really feel

NEGATIVE SPLIT

One thing I have always been challenged with in my running career is achieving a negative split in races, that is, running the second half of the race faster than the first half. My tendency is to pick a target time and then start off at a pace that will get me in a few minutes ahead. These few minutes I call my "slippage time." So far, it has worked for me but I think I could have done better if I had started off slower and then picked it up. I read somewhere that for every one minute you run faster in the first half of a race you'll run two minutes slower in the second half of a race. Note to self: try harder to follow the plan in future races!

BOSTON QUALIFIERS

In Canada, certain marathons are Boston Qualifiers. This means they have been measured and certified by Athletics Canada. In fact there are 58 certified courses in the country including the Cochrane Foothill Marathon route. Victoria is one of them, too, and my time in that race in October allowed me to qualify for Boston 2011. I received many e-mails congratulating me and asking me what my training schedule had been to achieve this result. It was very simple really:

- no interval training
- no tempo runs
- no hill repeats
- 187 long slow runs

that the foothills were starting to slip into that part of fall that feels a lot more like winter. On October 15 I woke up to the first snowstorm of the year. That day, I ran at Cochrane High School, with a variety of students on a snow-covered field. One, Grade 10 student Brandon, made some adjustments to his class schedule so he could run with me – he ended up going the farthest he had ever run, a half-marathon at 21.1 km. I'd run with over 8,000 kids thus far that year and Brandon took the cup for most kilometres run with me by a student!

By the end of October I had decided I would try to visit 60 schools as part of Marathon Quest 250. I put some feelers out there, via my blog, to ensure that I could do so. Brandon's school was number 43. I had come to realize that one of the main reasons I was managing to continue with the quest was the school runs. When I initially asked Sue to book the schools, my thinking was that it would be great to involve children and do some fundraising for RTP. What I didn't realize was how they would feed my spirit.

I knew that I could make it week to week if I had a school visit planned. No matter how down I felt as I drove to a school, everything changed when I started to talk to the kids in an assembly. I'd then head out and start running around their sports field and they would join me. Students from kindergarten to Grade 12 all had a story to tell and they all wanted to be part of something. Sue always said that the school runs were my happiest times, and she couldn't wait to hear about them. It's true. I always had stories about what the children had done and said and how they had made it all worthwhile.

When Monday, October 25, arrived, I finally awoke to the day I'd been thinking about for months: Marathon 200. During the summer and early fall, when I was injured and running in the rain, I kept saying to myself, "Get me to 200." I was finally there. By this point I had helped secure $115,317.88 for Right To Play and I'd run 8,440 km.

SHOES

Running shoes were a critical part of Marathon Quest 250. At the beginning, I tried contacting a number of manufacturers to see if any of them were interested in sponsoring me. I had no luck. In the end, one manufacturer (Salomon), two individuals and seven sports stores help me to get the 25 pairs I needed for the year. I used one pair for every 10 marathons. By the end of the quest I had run in nine different makes and 20 different models.

The 25 pairs of shoes I used during the quest were:

Pearl Izumi: Sky Dex, Asics Gel Cumulus 9 (2 pairs), Asics Gel 1110, Asics Gel Cumulus 10, Brooks Glycerin, Asics Hinsei 2, Salomon Gore-Tex XT Wings (3 pairs), Saucony Ride 2, New Balance 1062 (2 pairs), Asics Gel Cumulus 11, Adidas Supernova Glide, Mizuno Wave Creation II, New Balance 1906, New Balance 1064, Etonic Praya, Salomon XT Wings 2 (2 pairs), Asics Gel 1140, New Balance: Trail, Brooks Adrenaline and Brooks Cascadia. By Marathon 196 I had only sustained four blisters! Following is my roll of honour for everyone who helped me keep the rubber on the road!

- Myself, Marathon Quest 250 (3 starter pairs)
- Francis, Salomon (5 pairs)
- Mark, Trailblazers Store, Cochrane (3 pairs)
- Elaine, *Impact Magazine*, Calgary (3 pairs)
- Sandy, New Balance Store, Calgary (3 pairs)
- Jack, Fast Trax Running and Ski Store, Edmonton (2 pairs)
- Mark, The Edge Sports Store, Cochrane (2 pairs)
- Gord, Gord's Running Store, Calgary (1 pair)
- Jeremy, Strides Running Store, Calgary (1 pair)
- Ian, The Tech Shop, Calgary (1 pair)
- Sherrie, Professional Coaches, Calgary (1 pair)

#190 made up of 19 used pairs of shoes.

I spent some time with media on this day, doing interviews with Jim Brown on CBC's *Eyeopener* before meeting Kevin Green from CTV at Eau Claire Market. I planned to run a 10 km out and back course, then start the next loop at 10:30 a.m. I headed west along the Bow and at the 4.5 km mark I passed a sign warning people about coyotes. I had been this way dozens of times and never really took notice of the sign. This time I should have. I had run only about 20 more metres down the path when I saw a coyote cross the path, then disappear. I made my way with Spidey senses tingling to the turnaround point, then beat a hasty retreat to the cafe. Coyotes are not to be trifled with, especially when running alone.

Reporters from CBC TV, the Canadian Press and the *Calgary Herald* caught up with me before I'd finished the marathon. It was a good day, a bit nippy, but fine running weather. The 200th was made more special by the people who sponsored it: Tom and Lyle. Tom, of course, had introduced me to Right To Play, and we had been in contact all year about the fundraiser. Tom and his wife, Ulrica, had moved from Calgary to Fredericton, New Brunswick, in June 2010. I had been in contact with him continuously and he

A MILITARY SECRET

A number of magazine and newspaper articles came out about Marathon Quest 250 after Marathon 200. One piece that caught my eye was on CBCnews.com. The article described the quest and Right To Play – it was a solid report. What really drew me to this piece of media, however, were the comments below the article. Here are a few of them:

- Very inspiring, just goes to show that there are good people out there that are willing to "go the extra mile" for kids.
- Wow... that's 5,000 miles, isn't it? Or equivalent to running coast to coast?
- Fifteen minutes of fame takes an awful lot of running these days to achieve.
- This guy will die before he finishes marathon #250. What a waste.
- Watch him have a heart attack at some point; studies have proven that marathoners wear out their hearts.
- Marathons are extremely hard on the body, especially the knees; unless he's using some kind of special shoes and knee braces, he must have a body the military would drool over to study.
- I know, with multi-marathon runners, they all say the trick is to keep eating. Some friends I know wear two belts, one for water bottles, the other just for potatoes. The starch apparently keeps them going.

I decided I would have to give the potato belt a try. I didn't really worry about the military storming my house, though.

had been drumming up support in eastern Canada. Lyle was also connected in my mind to my reasons for raising money for RTP, as he and his wife, Christa, had completed the Tour d'Afrique in 2006.

In November, as fall came to a close, the mornings turned decidedly chilly. Despite this, I continued to stop in at MacKay's for ice cream when I completed marathons in Cochrane. My goal of eating all 47 flavours at MacKay's before the year's end seemed to be in sight until November 6, when I found out that I had been operating under the delusion that there were 47 fixed flavours. Turns out that Cochrane's world-class ice creamery has 42 fixed flavours and then five others that they switch up, which meant they could keep bringing out new flavours and I might never succeed in trying them all. I decided to keep eating ice cream anyway, even after the hard frost we received on November 9. It was time to bring out the winter woollies – perhaps even the hand warmers – but not time to give up MacKay's sweet and tasty cones!

Remembrance Day was also cold. Within five minutes the hose on my hydration pack had frozen. I realized I needed to winterize the nozzle again, bring out my as yet unpatented Nozzle Warmer-upper. I ran with a friend, Andrew, and we headed out, down to Spray Lake Sawmills Family Sports Centre in Cochrane, then over to the community cenotaph near the Cochrane Legion. The area was packed with civilians, as well as members of the armed forces and veterans. We all observed a moment of silence, thinking about wars past and present and the soldiers taken by those wars, thinking about the possibility of peace in our time.

The snow soon began to fall, so I tried to keep my marathons confined to Cochrane to avoid icy roads and white-knuckle drives. Of course, some days I had to hop in my car to get to a school, but otherwise I kept the running local! On November 19 I checked the thermometer at the beginning of Marathon 220 and it read −28°c. I had to layer up: three sets of running tights, five layers on

CONFLICT RESOLUTION AND PEACE BUILDING, THE RIGHT TO PLAY WAY

"You don't wait for peace in order to use sport for peace. You can use sport to achieve peace." –Shimon Peres, Athens Roundtable on Sport for Development and Peace, 2004

Right To Play varies the programs it delivers to kids in communities abroad, but it focuses all of its programs on four impact development areas: Basic Education and Child Development, Health Promotion and Disease Prevention, Community Development and Participation, and Conflict Resolution and Peace Building.

Children from communities that have been torn apart by conflict benefit from participating in regular activities that help them heal. Right To Play encourages vulnerable youth to participate in sport programs at critical moments in their lives, helping them fill a void and reducing the likelihood that they will go on to engage in violent behaviour.

Sport alone cannot prevent war, but it can contribute to bigger peace-building efforts. Palestinian schools, for example, implementing RTP curriculum, have fewer occurrences of violence amongst their students. Right To Play has been involved with the Global Peace Games for children and youth that have been hosted all over the world since 2001. RTP also puts together special tournaments and friendly competitions within the communities it serves to bring "opposites" together in order to expose kids to nonviolence, mutual respect and friendly competition. Right To Play has found that when people engage in inclusive sport and play, tensions relax and barriers break down: collaboration happens. Sport creates a space that allows peace to take root.

top, two sets of gloves, balaclava, toque, mask and ski goggles. The biggest issue continued to be my hydration pack. If I didn't take a drink every four minutes, the nozzle would freeze solid. That day, I decided to stay close to home and pop in when I wanted to warm up. My 1.25 km loop worked well, and I had completed 21.1 km by 12:00 p.m. Of course, the other issue I started to encounter again as I ran through the cold was constantly fogging goggles!

I couldn't believe it when, four days later, on November 23, conditions got even worse. On that day, the temperature was –41°c. cbc Radio announced that Calgary was the second-coldest place on Earth after the South Pole. Bearing in mind that skin freezes if exposed to –44° for one minute, I layered up again and set out. I figured this weather would be good training for Yellowknife: Sue and I were set to head up north on November 26 to run Marathon 224 in my old stomping grounds in the Northwest Territories. I was to run at St. Patrick's and Sir John Franklin High Schools. WestJet had sponsored this trip, and I was grateful and excited to return to the North, even though I knew that temperatures might be pretty grim.

On the Thursday morning, before the marathon, Sue and I boarded a WestJet flight arriving in Yellowknife in the early afternoon, where we would stay with my old friend Gerard, his wife, Cathy, and their children, Nick, Jessica and Suzanne. The first thing we heard about was a fuel crisis: the ice roads were not yet ready and fuel tankers that usually were able to drive to Yellowknife at this time of year were unable to reach the city. It turned out that Yellowknife's conditions, at –21°c, were much better than southern Alberta's had been! We visited St. Patrick and Sir John Franklin schools that afternoon, and I talked to the students about the quest. Then it was back to Gerard and Cathy's to get ready for the next day's run.

On Friday morning, Gerard shuttled me around to some media interviews before the start of the marathon. The sun rose at 9:30 a.m. and set at 3:30 p.m. – not a big window in which to complete a marathon. Soon we were at St. Patrick's, where a number of teachers and students from both schools joined me on 1 km loops around the school. The route around the school was getting a bit boring, so in the afternoon a group of us headed down to Old Town and the Dene First Nation community of N'dilo on Latham Island. I love the rugged beauty of this part of Canada. The float–ski planes parked along the shoreline in the city reminded me that Yellowknife is still a frontier community.

END OF SEASON STATS TO DATE

BEST QUESTION POSED BY A CHILD: "Who is your competition?"
PRODUCT OF THE SEASON: Acupuncture
NUMBER OF MARATHONS: 226
NUMBER OF MARATHON RACES: 6
DISTANCE COVERED: 9537.2 km
NUMBER OF STEPS TAKEN: 11,732,700
NUMBER OF SHOES USED: 22 pairs
EQUIVALENT FLIGHT DISTANCE: Calgary to Aganan, Guam
NUMBER OF SCHOOLS / DAY CAMPS VISITED: 51
AMOUNT OF MONEY RAISED FOR RTP: $141,826.97
NUMBER OF CHILDREN WHO RAN WITH ME: 10,179
AVATAR "MARATHON MARTIN": Ellensburg, Washington

12

WINTER AGAIN: THE QUEST COMES TO A CLOSE

"Success is sweet and sweeter if long delayed
and gotten through many struggles and defeats."

—ANONYMOUS

Imagine that you've spent 11 months running marathons five days a week. You are exhausted, but you are finally at month 12, the last month during which you need to run the marathons. You feel like racing toward the end, but then you decide to savour every last one of the marathons, knowing that this special series of runs will never come again.

The final month of the quest dawned clear and crisp. My first three December marathons were at schools. I continued to work toward the "quest-within-a-quest": School Quest 60. First, West Dover School, followed by Dr. J.K. Mulloy and Heritage Christian Academy, all in Calgary. At West Dover I met an especially curious set of students who had studied my website carefully and had questions that ranged from the everyday "Where were you born?" (one girl asked me this question about 10 times) to the health-conscious "How healthy is poutine?" It was a great group. One particular student in Grade 6, Jach (pronounced "Josh"), really made me think. During the morning, he ran with me on several loops around the playground and we talked. Six years ago, Jach and his family had immigrated to Canada from the Sudan, and he was slowly getting used to his new life. The bell rang and he went back to class. Later, he approached me at the end of my run and gave me $3.95 for Right To Play. He had perhaps a more intimate understanding than some of his classmates of what Right To Play programs might mean for kids in conflict-torn or poverty-stricken areas.

RIGHT TO PLAY IN CANADA

Although Right To Play operates in countries far from my home in Canada, it also brings programs to kids right in my backyard. In June 2010 the charity launched the Promoting Life-skills in Aboriginal Youth (PLAY) program in partnership with Moose Cree First Nation and Sandy Lake First Nation in Ontario. PLAY's goal is to build on the strengths of Aboriginal youth in their communities, include elders and their teaching and support the values of culture and identity. As well as all RTP programs, PLAY will be tailor-made for each Aboriginal community it enters, because it will be designed in each community and based on individual community needs. Wherever PLAY is, however, it will deliver the following four programs: Summer Sun (a summer day camp including youth and elders and focusing on behaviour management, culture, safety and local concerns); Youth Leadership; After School (for elementary-school kids); and Hockey for Development.

Two-time gold medal Olympic hockey player Sami Jo Small spent some time as an RTP athlete ambassador at Sandy Lake in 2011. She was impressed with RTP's work in the community, happy to be there to help and especially proud that she was able to teach the girls of Sandy Lake how to play hockey. "Sport isn't life, but it teaches you a lot about yourself," she said. By the time Sami Jo was in Sandy Lake, PLAY had extended its operations into 39 First Nations communities and had become a leadership program that affected over 1,000 kids.

Running with the kids on marathon #227 at West Dover School.

After getting the three school runs in, Sue and I flew to Las Vegas for my last "official" marathon of the year. To recap, here are the dates of the official events, their Marathon Quest numbers and my chip times:

Boston	April 19	065	4:42:41	
Vancouver	May 2	074	5:06:45	
Red Deer	May 23	089	4:40:51	
Calgary	May 30	094	4:34:18	
Regina	September 12	167	5:48:47	
Victoria	October 10	188	3:43:43	(Boston Qualifier!)
Las Vegas	December 5	229	4:40:51	

I'm not sure what happened in Victoria. It must have been the afternoon tea and the cucumber sandwiches I had enjoyed at the Empress Hotel the day before.

We travelled on the Friday and then spent most of Saturday working our way through Las Vegas to the race expo. It sounded as if it should have been a simple walk from our hotel: head down the strip to the Sands Convention Centre. However, as in life, things are not as simple as they sound. We left the Luxor at 9:00 a.m. and walked through to the Excalibur. Then we proceeded across the strip to the MGM. We took a monorail ride to Harrah's, through an underground parking lot to the Venetian, then walked on to the Sands. Whew. Las Vegas is a "rock 'n' roll" marathon known for its live bands, cheerleaders and themed water stations, and the expo was hopping. After we picked up our T-shirts and timing chip we spotted a sign for Scott Jurek, who was signing posters. Having read so much about Scott and watched the movie *The Distance of Truth*, it was a pleasure meeting him.

On the Saturday night, I had a surprise treat in store for Sue. I had managed to get tickets to see Andrea Bocelli. He was performing at the MGM Grand for one night only. He is Sue's favourite singer, and she was thrilled to actually see him perform live.

Sunday was an early start. There were about 29,000 runners, and I was in corral #20. A Cher impersonator sang the American national anthem and a Blues Brothers tribute band got everyone pumped up. The gun went off at 7:00 a.m. and the corral starts were one minute apart. There were great sights along the course. Running along the strip, I passed the Luxor, MGM Grand, Bellagio, Mirage and Treasure Island hotels. At the 5 km mark I passed Sponge Bob Square Pants Elvis. Things were going well. The half-marathon route was up the strip and back, and then the marathoners turned west toward the desert for the second half. I had made pretty good time, but on the last 200 m I was overtaken by an Elvis impersonator and a couple dressed as newlyweds.

I felt I had reached a milestone after running the last official marathon of the year, but I also knew I had to hammer home a few more runs and finish up a couple more quests. Another of my quests-within-a-quest continued to be my MacKay's marathon. By this point, I had decided to go for a 50-flavour quest, regardless of the new flavours the ice creamery dreamed up along the way. On December 10, Marathon 233, I consumed the final flavour in my ice cream quest: candy cane.

The ice cream board at MacKay's. A taste bonanza.

FAVOURITE MACKAY'S FLAVOURS

When I started my ice cream quest, kids asked me what my favourite flavours were. They also wanted to know which ones I really thought were the worst. Following are the top three in both categories:

FIVE-STAR FLAVOURS	DEFINITELY NOT MY FAVES
Coconut Delight	Bubble Gum
Tropical Mango	Licorice
White Chocolate Raspberry Truffle	Root Beer

Chatting with students at Abbeydale School before marathon #236.

On Marathon 237 I hit 10,000 km, and the next day I finished up School Quest 60. The first school was Mount View on January 7, Marathon 006, and the temp was −31°c. The last school marathon, 238, was also at Mount View. Talk about coming full circle! This time the temperature was a toasty −19°c. In between, I had run at schools in Calgary, Cochrane, Airdrie, Exshaw, Canmore, Okotoks and Yellowknife. In total I had run with over 12,000 students from kindergarten to Grade 12. I'd run on pathways around the school, in parks, on soccer fields, even a 100 m strip of pavement in front of one school. I'd told kids about my bike trip across Africa, how I'd played soccer with children in the Sudan and table tennis with kids in Ethiopia. Of course, I also told them about Right To Play programs all over the world, including Canada. And what did the kids do? They gave me their pocket money to "help the other kids."

Mount View students, during that last school marathon, were no different. I chatted with the children at assembly then I started running. A number of them remembered me from my previous visit and said hello. It was a busy day. The kids were preparing their Christmas concert, *A Charlie Brown Christmas*. When I asked them if they wanted me to re-enact the part when Charlie Brown (me) tries to kick the football and Lucy takes it away, they said, politely, "No."

At this point, so close to the end of the quest, I was sometimes running six marathons a week. This was because, back in the summer, I had been forced to switch to Plan B in order to ensure I could run all 250 marathons within the year. I was running on some of what I had hoped would be off days, and was starting to feel totally fatigued. Also, Sue was becoming increasingly concerned about my physical state, though she didn't tell me this at the time! I perked up a bit when my fellow Red Rock Running Club member Leslie showed me the latest issue of *Canadian Running* in which were recorded the 2010 Golden Shoe Awards. The magazine had awarded me a golden shoe for "Mega Marathons!" Every week, Sue and I speak to our granddaughter Autumn, and when I told her she was very excited and wanted to know how to get a golden shoe. We decided to get a little running shoe, spray-paint it gold and send it to her as a surprise for all her running efforts. As you might imagine, she was thrilled.

Receiving my award pulled me through to my 55th birthday, which happened just before Marathon 241. I had made it to the final countdown!

As I moved through the final 10 marathons of the quest, I found myself speeding up. I was completing marathons in less than five hours. During this time, members of the Cochrane community were helping me to plan for the final marathon. Robin at Spray Lake Sawmills Family Sport Centre had really pulled out the stops. Tim Horton's and Coca Cola would supply drinks, Cochrane Toyota would bring a burger mobile, and Mark at Trailblazers would be there to hold a raffle. Best of all, Robin had lined up three bouncy castles, of which I am a great fan.

Marathon 247 saw me running with my friend Florin again in Calgary. I had met him on the pathways way back in June, and had been running with him off and on ever since. When I was feeling like I was a bit crazy, Florin had reassured me of my sanity. I trusted him because he had a PhD in psychology. I knew I would soon be speaking with Tony Harris of CNN again, whose first question to me back in December 2009 had been "Are you nuts?" When I met up with Florin, I asked him about my mental health again, and again he reassured me that I was just fine. Thanks, Florin.

DEVELOPING LEADERSHIP SKILLS THE RTP WAY: PROTECTOR DODGEBALL

If you can support others, you have the makings of a good leader. We all have bad memories about brutal games of dodgeball in school, but Right To Play participants have fantastic memories about playing Protector Dodgeball. This game helps kids think about the people who protect and support them and how those people work as leaders and mentors.

To play this game, kids stand in a circle facing inward. Three volunteers form a line in the middle of the circle, spread out and then stretch their arms out to their sides to touch the shoulders of the person in front of them. The first person in the line is the protector, and he or she must protect the two players behind him or her as children in the circle take turns gently throwing a soft ball at them. The protector is allowed to catch the ball, or he or she can block it to make sure it doesn't hit the other two in the centre.

Once everyone has had a turn "dodging" the ball, coaches ask the kids to think about what it felt like to be the protector and what they did to protect the others. Then coaches encourage the kids to think about someone in their own lives who is a "protector" and how that person makes them feel safe. A conversation ensues about how kids might apply "protector" skills to become protectors themselves, role models, mentors for others.

The end was in sight, and I was starting to see how media attention could really help me raise money for Right To Play. On Marathon 248, with only two to go and having raised $181,701.50 of the $250,000-goal, *National Post* reporter Megan O'Toole told me I should pick up a copy of the paper because an article on the quest would be there. She didn't tell me it was on the front page! When I went home to check my e-mail, I found 46 donations. Normally, I get between two and three per day. I wondered if my interview with Tony Harris would help raise some funds as he had suggested it would back in December 2009. I was starting to worry I wouldn't meet my goal.

Reflecting on how we felt the night before the last marathon, Sue admits she was looking forward to MQ 250 being over. It had been a long year and at times our lives didn't seem to be our own. She thought we would "get back to normal, whatever normal is." Little did she know!

December 31 dawned bright and cold, −27°C. The course Robin and I had worked out was a 2 km out-and-back along the Bow River. At 9:00 a.m. 30 of us headed out. We were blowing steam as we turned west. My hydration pack was already starting to freeze, but I kept taking sips every couple of minutes to keep the liquid flowing. The world around us looked stunningly beautiful. Frost covered everything: trees, rocks, vegetation, dogs, humans. Our hair became white and spiky as we ran; eyebrows and beards had chunks of ice forming in them. All the while, the river bubbled and ice mist rolled along amongst the mini icebergs.

Camera crews from CTV, CBC and Global joined us, taking up strategic positions along the riverbank. Sandy and Jody from the town of Cochrane had found some old signs in a warehouse and placed them along the route. My favourite was "Viva Las Cochrane." At 10:30 I got my call from Tony Harris of CNN. I was keen to tell him I wasn't crazy after all! As I chatted with him, I could hardly hear and I was freezing cold. The other runners hung around. I told Tony that it was great to hear from him, and he said he was impressed that I had completed the quest. I asked him what the weather was like in Atlanta, and he said it was cold. In the end, I told him I was only a little bit nuts, before saying goodbye and moving on with my merry band of runners.

Global TV took some footage via a pickup truck going 7 km/h ahead of us. I had to stop them and tell them to move on. Wouldn't that have been a laugh – "Marathon Martin dies of carbon monoxide fumes on last marathon of 2010!" On lap seven we were joined by people riding a different kind of transportation: two horses came toward us, ridden by local councillor Ivan Davies on his horse Gunnar, along with a friend. The horses were steaming and covered in frost, but they stayed with us for several laps. By the time we completed the half-marathon, I was feeling a bit overwhelmed. A group of 100 fresh runners were waiting for us at the sport centre, ready for their half-marathon.

I took a break at this point and was able to meet Mike Dorion, a volunteer with Right To Play who had helped me on several other marathons during the year. People were lined up at the doors to make donations, and groups of runners were keeping warm with Tim Horton's coffee. By the time we headed out for the last half, the running group was up to 130 people. Some kids joined the gang too, and I recognized a few of them from my school runs. I was cheered to see so many kids at the final stage, running, laughing, cheering us on.

The day warmed up and so I had stripped off a layer at the half-time break. As we progressed, several of the marathoners started to have a hard time. A number of them were doing their first marathon, and fatigue started to catch up with them at the 30 km mark. I realized that each of us was on his or her own quest, but we were supporting each other. Look after yourself, look after one another.

At kilometre 32 I arrived back at the sports centre. The crowd was huge, full of people waiting to do a 10 km run with me. I took a

Above: Heading off at the start of marathon #250.
Below: An incredible morning, windless, with frost covering the trees.

Wearing my full winter gear. Only the eyes are showing.

five-minute break and grabbed a coffee and a burger, then I shouted, "30 seconds!" and we all shuffled outside. The crowd was pumped and I vocalized another countdown. I really was savouring each loop. It was odd, when I only had five more laps to go and realized I was coming to the end, I didn't want it to end. I gathered up the 5 km run group and gave a bunch of kids some high fives. When we had one lap to go, I still needed more distance to complete the marathon. I told the 300-plus crowd that I had to cross the bridge to run the last few kilometres, that they should wait for me on the other side.

I crossed the bridge and looked back across the river. So many people were waving and cheering. They were all there to celebrate.

It was at this moment I realized that, despite my being physically alone, everyone was with me in spirit.

Robin asked me if, at the end of this, my final run, I would enter the arena on my own. I knew this was not how I wanted to finish, so I rounded up a large group of kids and we all ran in together.

I was deeply moved to see the crowd that had gathered inside.

PHOTO: PATRICK PRICE

Running into the Sports Centre with a group of 30 kids at the end of marathon #250.

The group of people comprised not only my friends and family but also many members of the community. I was proud to receive an award in recognition of my achievement from our mayor, Truper McBride.

By the end of the day, Marathon Quest 250 had raised an extra $15,195.86 for Right To Play, bringing our total up to $208,036.50. And more was yet to come.

END OF SEASON STATS TO DATE

BEST QUESTION POSED BY A CHILD: "Where are you from?" x 10
PRODUCT OF THE SEASON: MacKay's Ice Cream
NUMBER OF MARATHONS: 250
NUMBER OF MARATHON RACES: 7
DISTANCE COVERED: 10,550.0 km
NUMBER OF STEPS TAKEN: 12,978,650
NUMBER OF SHOES USED: 25 pairs
EQUIVALENT FLIGHT DISTANCE: Calgary to Canton, China
NUMBER OF SCHOOLS / DAY CAMPS VISITED: 60
AMOUNT OF MONEY RAISED FOR RTP: $208,036.50.
NUMBER OF CHILDREN WHO RAN WITH ME: 12,032
AVATAR "MARATHON MARTIN": Back home in Cochrane, Alberta

13

COOL DOWN, CHECK IN, THEN COMRADES

"Take rest. A field that has rested gives a beautiful crop."

—OVID

It was over, and it was just beginning.

As we approached the end of 2010, Sue had talked about how I might feel when Marathon Quest 250 came to an end. Neither of us were sure how finishing might affect my body and my mind too. She suggested I give myself a goal: sign up for a future race, give myself something to aim for. At that point in the year, many people had already begun asking me what I was going to do in 2011.

I decided to book myself in for two other events in 2011: the Comrades ultramarathon on May 29 in South Africa, and my yearly appointment on September 14 with my urologist, Dr. Baverstock. Needless to say, I was more excited about Comrades than Dr. Baverstock. One of my running friends, Ken Skea, had already signed up for Comrades, and it would be fun running with someone I knew. The Comrades Marathon is an 89 km race and holds the Guinness World Record as the largest and oldest ultramarathon in the world, with 18,000 participants. It was good to have a goal.

Sue was right: the New Year presented me with a whole new scenario. The first two days were okay. After all, I was used to taking days off during my year of marathons. I happily ate bacon sandwiches on New Year's Day and the day after, and watched English soccer, without really knowing what to expect in the days to come.

Day 3 seemed okay too, maybe because we were still caught up in the thrill of my achievement, still reminiscing about the year and working on the fundraising. That day, Sue and I were out the door at 5:00 a.m. to attend to an early-morning media appointment with CBC Radio's *Eyeopener*. Jim Brown, the show's host, is a pro and makes his guests feel truly comfortable. He wanted to know how I was feeling and how the fundraising was coming along. By this point, Marathon Quest 250 had raised $212,000.

That afternoon, I was relaxing at home when I received a call from Steve Flewelling. I had worked for Steve in Sudbury several years before. He became senior vice-president of projects and exploration at Xstrata Nickel. Through the grapevine, he had heard about my quest and was interested in learning more. After we had caught up with one another, I told him about Right To Play. What he told me next really blew me away. Xstrata had decided they wanted to make a $30,000 donation to the cause. I was speechless. Xstrata's gift alone would allow 600 kids to receive Right To Play programs for one year. It seemed we might meet our goal after all.

As the final dollars came in and we got closer and closer to our $250,000 target, I booked myself in for a battery of tests to see what impact running 10,550 km over the course of one year had made on my body. Over the course of two weeks, starting on January 4, the following tests were conducted: blood and urine, thyroid, knees and hips scan, chest x-ray, bone density (via 3D bone imaging), echocardiogram and VO_2 max.

I've talked about the VO_2 max before. I underwent this test at the beginning of my year of marathons and again after 83 marathons. It measures the maximum capacity of an individual's body to transport and use oxygen during incremental exercise, and it reflects the physical fitness of the test subject. The "v" in the name stands for "volume per time"; O_2, of course, means oxygen; and "max," maximum. Again, my physiotherapist, Serge, conducted the VO_2 max test at his lab. He kitted me out with a mask and heart-rate monitor, and then he had me run myself to exhaustion on a treadmill, steadily increasing the pitch as I ran.

PHOTO: PATRICK PRICE

Undertaking a VO$_2$ max test at Cochrane Sport Physio.

The next big test I had was a 3D bone-imaging analysis, to check up on my bone density. At the beginning of the quest, some people told me my ankles would cave, my knees and hips would be destroyed and my leg bones fail, all because of the continual pounding of the pavement that the marathons required. Now, we would find out what damage was done. The analysis involved a variety of space-age tools. The first part of the test took place in a room right out of *Star Trek*. I had to lie on a bed while an overhead tracker completed a full-body bone scan. Then I walked down a floor to finish up the test on the Scanco Medical Xtreme CT 3D Bone Analyzer. I was instructed to sit down and then stick my right arm, then my right leg, into a hole. The analyzer then performed a 360° scan of my wrist and ankle, checking bone density and health. Of course, this scan was much easier on me than the VO_2 max test!

I wouldn't have my test results for a while, so I contented myself with working on the fundraising and trying to get back to "normal." I was starting to feel a bit at loose ends. The fundraising continued, but I was no longer attached to the schedule to which I had become so accustomed. I didn't even feel like running. Still, I decided that I should run 10 km each week just to keep the legs ticking over. At this point, I was still getting lots of calls from the media, so interviews still took up a lot of my time.

Then, in the middle of January, Sarah at Right To Play invited me to travel to Benin to visit some schools that were using RTP programs. She learned that I would be doing the Comrades ultra in May, so she organized my trip to Benin for after that event. I was thrilled. Later, in February, RTP made me an honorary athlete ambassador, and I found out I would be accompanying two other athlete ambassadors to Benin. The trip was a future event I could build on! I think knowing I was going there helped me continue on through the weird days of January 2011.

By January 17, we were all still working at meeting the target fundraising amount. But at 2:25 p.m. that day, Dr. Bill Hanlon gave me a call. He asked me how far we were from hitting our fundraising goal. With a precision born of working non-stop with the numbers of dollars and cents raised, I told him: $1,271.64. He generously covered this amount with a donation, which meant that, at 2:30 p.m., the donation-to-date figure on Marathon Quest 250's blog read $250,000. I felt a sense of relief and disbelief. I had reached my goal. Five thousand children would receive Right To Play programming in 2011.

One weekend toward the end of January, the local Rotary Club invited me to become a member of the Raucous Rotary Relics in the Kimmett Cup. This meant I would have to strap on my skates for the first time in 10 years, but I was more than happy to do it for this very worthy cause.

The Kimmett Cup is held every year in memory of a brilliant young woman named Lindsay Kimmett. She was a promising medical student and hockey player who tragically died in 2008. She had been a passenger in a car that turned over as she was on her way home from a hockey game. The Kimmetts are a highly regarded local family. The event raises donations for the Lindsay Leigh Kimmett Foundation. The foundation supports enduring valedictorian scholarships at all three Cochrane high schools; the Dr. Lindsay Leigh Kimmett Prize in Emergency Medicine at the University of Calgary Medical School, and Lindsay's Kids Minor Hockey & Ringette Sponsorships. As well, the foundation's flow-through fund makes significant donations to a variety of efforts, including local recreation and sports, Red Cross relief in Haiti and Marathon Quest 250.

The Kimmett Cup is a series of hockey games, played by the Kimmett family and their friends together with members of the local community and beyond. We began at 8:00 a.m. on Mitford Pond. As the sun came up, the puck was dropped and the game was on. After a long day of scrimmages, and much fun, I fell asleep exhausted. It was the kind of exhaustion I had been used to in 2010. The next morning, my muscles were screaming. It felt good to have taken part. There was something about having a physical goal, moving toward it, and doing some good in the process, that had me hooked and made me realize I wanted to do more of the same.

Also in January, I returned to Glenbow School in Cochrane, where I had run Marathon 184 back in early October 2010. It was great to be back and say hi to the kids. A winter sports day was in full swing, and the students had been trying a variety of events: hockey, curling, bobsledding, snowshoeing and luging. I was there to chat with them about Marathon Quest 250. They didn't know that some very special guests would also be there to help me out.

At 12:55 p.m. a minivan pulled up and three Right To Play representatives emerged: Jamie Wilson, Sarah Stern and Julia Myer

THE NUMBERS

I love statistics, and Marathon Quest 250 generated loads of them. Here are just a few:

Distance:
- marathon distance: 42.2 km (26.2 miles)
- number of marathons: 250
- total distance run: 10,550 km (6,550 miles)

Time:
- total running time: 61 days 9 hours, 56 minutes, 50 seconds
- average time for one marathon: 5:53:45
- first 125 marathons: 30 days, 13 hours, 14 minutes, 31 seconds
- second 125 marathons: 30 days, 20 hours, 32 minutes, 19 seconds
- not a negative split!

from head office in Toronto. With them were Irene and Asana, two RTP coaches from Ghana, who had arrived in Canada the day before. A presentation full of music and information followed. Julia talked about what RTP does overseas, and the Ghanaian women talked about their work with children in their local community. They explained how they used RTP programs to teach the children about leadership and community. Then I told the kids what I had been doing since the marathons.

At the time, RTP was carrying out a cross-Canada awareness campaign: first stop, Calgary. Sarah told me the organization would be hosting an awareness event at MacEwan Hall at the

Visiting Glenbow School with Right To Play representatives Irene and Asana from Ghana.

University of Calgary on February 1. The coaches and representatives from Ghana would be giving a presentation, as would one of RTP's athletic ambassadors, Olympic gold medalist Hayley Wickenheiser, who would talk about her experiences with RTP. Sarah asked me to say a few words about Marathon Quest 250. I agreed, of course.

By February 4 the donations to Marathon Quest 250 had risen to $287,231.73, enabling 5,745 kids to have RTP programming in 2011. That same week, I continued on the junket with RTP and the Ghanaians and joined Jamie, Sarah and Athlete Ambassador and Olympic gold medallist cross-country skier Beckie Scott to speak to a group from Samsung. Beckie shared her experiences with RTP in Ethiopia. The group, minus Beckie, then headed up to Edmonton and visited Mother Teresa, Bishop Savaryn and Monsignor William Irwin schools. The week caught me up in a whirlwind of presentations. Irene and Asana were enjoying their first visit to Canada. They had arrived during the winter and had never been so cold, but they did get a kick out of their first experience of snow.

When RTP moved on to other parts of Canada, I knew it was time for me to refocus. I needed to get down to some serious training for the Comrades ultra in May. I was way behind in my training. I should have put in 239 km in January, and I only did 40. I knew I had to pick up the pace if I wanted to complete the 89 km in the 12 hours allowed. However, I was reluctant to train outdoors when the weather was severe. I'd had enough of training in freezing temperatures the year before! So I jumped on the treadmill for the first time since 2009 – it was fun to put in 10 km while watching the Rangers vs. Celtic soccer cup tie.

As I started to ramp up my training, the results came in from the medical tests conducted in January. There was a lot of medical terminology in the reports, so I've paraphrased and added in some points of clarification:

Chest: Appears within normal limits. The heart is normal in size, the lungs and pleural space are clear with no active intrathoracic disease detected. *Meaning: Looks good.*

Hips: Appear well maintained. No significant degenerative changes identified. Bony pelvis is unremarkable. *Who says it's unremarkable!*

Knees: Shows good maintenance of joint space with no specific arthropathy apparent. No joint fluid or radiopaque loose bodies. No acute fracture or dislocation. *Meaning: Not bad for an old fella.*

Bone density: Researcher John Schipilow at the University of Calgary stated, "Overall, I would say your bone health is very good. I was not surprised by the results, mainly for the tibia. The one thing that really surprised me was the values for your radius. I did not think they would be as high as the tibia, but your wrist bones were looking a lot better than I expected. My initial thoughts are that there may be some sort of whole-body effects occurring with your extreme lifestyle over the past year." *Meaning: Further tests would be carried out in six months and again after one year. Stay tuned.*

Heart: Normal left ventricular size, wall motion and wall thickness with an estimated left ventricular ejection fraction of approximately 60 per cent. No other significant abnormality is identified. *Meaning: The ticker's still going.*

I was pleased with the results of the tests, even though I knew I would have to be subjected to more. It made it easier for me to continue with my training for Comrades knowing I was in good physical condition.

In early March I headed off to Toronto for the Prospectors and Developers Conference. Tom had asked me come out and talk to representatives of the mining industry about Right To Play. For two days I manned a booth and shared my story. It was a great experience, but the really mindset-changing event happened when I gave an interview to Supreme Master TV. Several weeks before arriving in Toronto, I had been told I had been awarded $10,000 from the Supreme Master Ching Hai Foundation for Marathon Quest 250. Supreme Master Ching Hai is a noted spiritual teacher and philanthropist who completes humanitarian work around the world.

At the end of the interview, I was given the cheque. As I shook hands with the interviewer, I thought of a person who has been a great inspiration to me: Clara Hughes. I remembered that Clara had donated $10,000 to RTP after winning gold in speed skating in the 2006 winter Olympics in Turin. As I exited the interview, I made a decision. I handed the cheque over to Robert Witchel and RTP. I was thrilled to be able to somewhat emulate Clara's gesture. I was, of course, humbled to receive the money from the foundation, and it gave me great pleasure put it to use where need was great.

The afternoon before returning to Cochrane, I met with Robert and Sarah. I told them I had a plan, sort of. I had decided I would try to raise $1-million for RTP over a five-year period. I wasn't sure yet how I would do it, but I was determined to try.

Returning to Cochrane, I continued to visit schools, which were still holding fundraisers for RTP. One of these visits involved a rather "sticky situation." In March 2011 St. Timothy School was holding a "Stick Up for Right To Play" fundraiser and I was the celebrity guest. I was able to cross off "hang from a gym wall by means of duct tape" from my bucket list. On the count of three, the "stick up" began. A quickly assembled team of teachers started to plaster duct tape across my body. In 15 minutes nine students and one marathon man were hanging off the walls of the gym. Then, after a few deft moves with scissors, I was on the ground again. By the end of the day, the teachers and students had raised $1,080 for Right To Play.

I was again amazed by kids' determination to host events and raise money for Right To Play. With the "stick-up" in mind, I mulled over a variety of ways in which I might meet my five-year, $1-million goal. Then it all seemed to come together when Julie Arnold from Netball Alberta asked me if I would help promote the game by playing against Earle Connor, the Paralympics sprinter and gold medallist. Julie was promoting our event as "The Hare vs. the Tortoise" – definitely cheeky. Earle and I joined members of the Women's U18 and U23 squads and played for two 15-minute periods. It was a tough game with lots of stops and starts; after the half-hour, I was done!

Through the fog of exhaustion after the netball game, I started to think. If that game had been six or 12 hours long, maybe I'd have had a chance! It's hard to explain what I was considering as I pondered my experiences with netball. Slowly, the idea of breaking Guinness World Records for different sports stuck in my head as a possible way to raise money for RTP. The next day, I asked Julie if Netball Alberta might be interested in an attempt to break the Guinness World Record for the longest netball game ever played. Julie didn't hesitate; she was all for it and said she would immediately take it to the executive and see what they said. The wheels were in motion.

It made me feel good that I would have a plan to return to after my trip to Africa. The Comrades and my trip to Benin were fast approaching, but I had one last event to complete, this time at Redwood Meadows, just outside Bragg Creek, Alberta. The activity was a 5 km fun run that would raise money for Redwood Meadows Children's Programming and Right To Play. Carol Scarratt was the event organizer, and she was in earnest: she netted 42 sponsors and some great prizes. Forty-five adults and 42 kids signed up ahead of time for the run, but by the time the event took place, over 130 adults and kids were involved. Unfortunately, the mosquitoes were out and involved too!

I ran with Sue, Jeremy and a young lad named Zac, who was running his first 5 km event, and he really wanted to finish. When Zac started having a tough time and wanted to quit, I stayed with him and I suggested we do walk breaks. These have always worked for me, and they worked for Zac too. We crossed the line in 41:37. Both Zac and his mom were thrilled. I have to say I felt pretty good too. That "coaching" experience and the $1,000 raised for the two organizations sounded a positive note and put me in good spirits for the Comrades.

The first Comrades Marathon race took place on May 24, 1921, founded by Vic Clapham, a First World War veteran. He started the race to honour South African soldiers killed during the war. Each year, the organizers alternate the route. One year it is uphill, from Durban to Pietermaritzburg, and the next year it's downhill the other way. This year, the course would run uphill.

At 6:00 p.m. on Tuesday, May 24, I gave Sue a big hug at the Calgary airport and boarded a plane for London Heathrow. Two days later, at 10:00 a.m. on Thursday morning, I landed in Durban. The next two days I rested.

At 3:00 a.m. on Sunday, May 29, I met up with my running buddy, Ken Skea, in the Polo Room of the Durban Hilton for a pre-race breakfast. Ken was working in India and it was great to see him again. I eat the same breakfast before any race: oatmeal, honey and a banana. The plan was to leave the hotel at 4:45 a.m. and make our way over to City Hall, two blocks away. As we headed to the start line, we overheard participants complaining about how cold it was. The temperature was 15°C, which is a pleasant summer's day in Cochrane. If only it had stayed that way!

The race had 16,000 starters and the streets were packed with people trying to get to the start line. Ken and I were seeded in Section D, and we were jammed into our corral like sardines. At

NETBALL

In 1891 James Naismith, a Canadian physical education teacher working in Massachusetts, invented basketball. The new game was quickly championed in the U.S. When basketball spread to England in 1893, it morphed when Martina Bergman-Österberg introduced a type of basketball to her female students at the Physical Training College in Hampstead. Over several years, basketball became "netball": the game moved outdoors and was played on grass; the baskets were replaced by rings that had nets.

Over 20 million people in more than 70 countries now play netball. The game is played in world championships and at the Commonwealth Games as well as the Olympics.

5:15 a.m. the crowd started singing "Shosholoza," a folksong sung by Ndebele migrants from Zimbabwe who worked in South Africa's mines. Some people call it South Africa's "second national anthem." After that, "Chariots of Fire" started to blare out of the loudspeakers. At 5:30, as the cock crowed, we set off to run the 86th Annual Comrades Marathon.

I had 12 hours to complete the 89 km from Durban to Pietermaritzburg, and I felt good. Ken and I started off together, but I knew it wouldn't be long before he would pull away. I maintained a good pace and the kilometres clicked by. The weather forecast had predicted a clear and sunny day, so I wore my "Martin of Arabia" hat with its neck flap. I was moving well and hit the halfway mark at 5:20:40.

During North American races, "pace bunnies" are used to help

Waiting at the start of the Comrades Marathon, singing "Shosholoza."

runners achieve a certain time. The "bunnies" are running volunteers who wear a pair of rabbit ears that are marked with the time at which they guarantee to get you over the finish line if you stay with them. Instead of bunnies, the Comrades has "buses," which are groups of people who will get you to the end within 10, 11 or 12 hours. I ran with the 11-hour bus, on and off, for the first 50 km, and I knew that if I stuck with it I'd be okay. At the 55 km mark, however, the wheels fell off my own "bus." It was getting hotter and hotter and my legs were starting to feel weak. The bus pulled away from me, and I never saw it again. For about 10 km I was in a dark place. I walked most of that distance and couldn't get myself going. Time was slipping away, and the possibility of missing the 12-hour cut-off was looming large.

At 65 km, however, a fellow behind me asked about the "Parnell 250" printed on the back of my shirt. I told him about Marathon

Quest 250, and he said I must be nuts. His name was Roy, from Johannesburg. He had completed nine Comrades races, and if he finished that day's run he would make it to ten, for which he would get a special medal. Two other runners were with him, Tony and Terrence. Running with this "mini-bus" picked up my spirits, and my pace improved. All along I was keeping in mind that if I came in any time after 12 hours, even if it was 12 hours and 1 second, I would receive no placing, no medal and no T-shirt. Now that is tough love.

It was going to be close for our little group. Roy was cramping up, and his pace was down to a slow shuffle. We entered the Pietermaritzburg Cricket Stadium at 11:49:00 and staggered forward for the last 400 m. The crowd was yelling and screaming, and our little band of comrades crossed the line at 11:51:23. Not a moment too soon!

Enjoying a Right To Play program with children at Vedoko School for the deaf in Benin, West Africa.

14
AND ON TO BENIN

"We make a living by what we get,
but we make a life by what we give."

—SIR WINSTON CHURCHILL

When Sarah first asked me to consider a trip to Benin in January 2011, I was thrilled. However, I knew virtually nothing about the country until I undertook some research. Benin was a French colony until 1960, at which time it gained full independence. It has a population of 9.3 million and is the size of Newfoundland. Its capital is Porto-Novo, and its largest city is Cotonou, where I would be going. The life expectancy of Benin citizens is 59 and the literacy rate is one of the lowest in the world, at 35 per cent. In fact, most children in Benin do not complete their primary-school education, and only slightly more than half of enrolled kids complete the fifth grade. I was interested to find out how Right To Play had affected kids in Benin, and I was on a high as I boarded the plane from Durban to Cotonou.

Right To Play has been in Benin since 2001, employing three core sports- and play-based education programs: Red Ball Child Play, Live Safe Play Safe, and Early Child Play. As well, in 2011, after piloting an ongoing teacher-training program, Right To Play joined with Benin's Ministry of Early Childhood & Primary Education to introduce an early childhood play-based curriculum for 80,000 children.

My introduction to Benin started on Monday, May 30, when I landed at the Cotonou airport and, upon stepping out of the plane, was hit by a wall of heat. It had been warm in Durban, but nothing prepared me for the furnace-like temperatures of Benin. Himi from Right To Play met me in the arrivals area and drove me to Hotel

Ibis. It was a hair-raising ride involving hundreds of motorbikes and scooters zipping around us and weaving in and out of the traffic. Fortunately I arrived in one piece.

That evening, I received a call to say that Robert Witchel, Caroline Ouellette and Heather Moyse had arrived, so I headed down to meet them. I had met Robert before and it was great to see him again. It was also a pleasure to meet Caroline and Heather, the two RTP athlete ambassadors who were also making the trip. We didn't stay up late talking, as we knew we had a long day ahead of us.

RTP'S PROGRAMS

Early Child Play is the name of RTP's programs for kids between the ages of 2 and 3, and 4 and 5. The programs include over 65 cooperative games that encourage holistic early childhood development. The games and activities help build kids' confidence, and are played using different coloured balls: red for development of the mind; black for development of the body; yellow for development of the spirit; blue for encouraging peace; and green for teaching about health. Programming for other age levels also uses the coloured ball scheme. Red Ball Child Play, for example, is geared toward ages 6 to 12.

Of course, RTP also provides a variety of programs for children that is not age-based, but thematic. For example, Abilities First is for kids from five to 18 years and encourages inclusion of children with disabilities. Live Safe Play Safe is, of course, RTP's HIV and AIDS education and prevention program, aimed toward three age groups ranging from six to nineteen. Youth As Leader embraces kids from 13 to 20, aiming to help kids develop knowledge and leadership skills, skills they can then bring to their communities.

HEATHER MOYSE AND CAROLINE OUELLETTE: RIGHT TO PLAY ATHLETE AMBASSADORS

Heather Moyse represented Canada in international competition as a bobsledder and a rugby union player. She won a gold medal in the two-woman competition at the 2010 Winter Olympics with Kaillie Humphries. She was also a member of the Canada national team and represented Canada at both the 2006 and the 2010 Women's Rugby World Cup. Before the trip to Benin as RTP athlete ambassador, Heather had spent three years in Trinidad and Tobago, developing and establishing a camp for deaf and hearing-impaired children.

Caroline Ouellette is a Canadian ice-hockey player and a member of the Canadian national women's hockey team, as well as a member of the Montreal Stars (CWHL). She is a three-time Olympic gold medallist, five-time winner of gold at the World Championships, a four-time winner of silver at the World Championships and a two-time Clarkson Cup Champion. Caroline is reputed to have one of the hardest shots in the women's game!

At 8:00 a.m. on May 31, Himi was waiting for us at the front door of Hotel Ibis. We left the air-conditioned splendour of the hotel and stepped out into the same heat I'd encountered the day before. Himi drove through the crazy rush-hour traffic to Right To Play's local offices, where we met Benin-born staff members Marie-Joséphine (country manager), Roméo Essou (program manager) and Christiane Boton (project coordinator). Marie-Joséphine talked about the work that Right To Play had been doing in the country, and she looked to the future: in 2011, RTP programs would reach over 167,000 children in 1,052 schools and

**Above: Robert and Caroline meet and play with children at Dogoudo Elementary School.
Below: Students present a traditional dance.**

48 youth centres. I was already blown away and I hadn't even visited a school yet.

Our first school visit was planned for that afternoon. Lunchtime traffic was no better than the morning's, but Himi is a gifted driver and we survived the trip. Dogoudo School teaches Grades 1 to 6 and has 295 students, but it only employs six teachers. I would find out as the trip progressed that the lack of teachers was a recurring theme. The school's three open-air classrooms verged on a large dirt courtyard. A group of Grade 5 and 6 boys and girls greeted us with a traditional dance, after which we dived straight into the games.

The first game we played was a team event with three teams of 10 members. We had to fill a ladle with water, run down a course, put the water in a pail, run back with the ladle and pass it to the next team member. I raced two Grade 4 kids and managed to win my heat. The kids loved this game and were yelling and cheering.

After the games, as Heather and Caroline played with a group of kids in the schoolyard, I was taken over to a set of drums and became part of the school band. The temperature was 35°c by this time, and I was soaked. The kids found this funny.

After saying goodbye, we were on the road again, heading out of Cotonou for a very special meeting. We had been granted an audience with King Allada xvi. Benin has 12 provinces, and there are several kings in each one. They still hold a lot of power over the local people, and Right To Play recognizes how important it is to get the kings to support its programs. With us were five children – three boys and two girls from five different schools – who were going to make a presentation to the king.

When we arrived at King Allada xvi's "palace," we entered a large room, stiflingly hot. We were shown to the comfy chairs, but the rest of the king's 70-strong entourage were seated on the floor. We waited. Then King Allada xvi entered and sat on his leopard-skin-covered throne. He was tall and looked regal. He wore a long green and brown tunic with a simple headpiece. He had a fan lady and an umbrella lady with him. A number of formal speeches were made in French, which unfortunately is not my strong suit. (I never had trouble with the kids, though, because I could communicate with gestures.)

We each had to introduce ourselves, so I'd learned "Je m'appelle Martin. Je suis coureur marathon," and that seemed to work. Then the kids gave their presentation on children's rights. They too delivered their speeches in French, but even for me their meaning was crystal clear. The room was hushed as the children stated that they had a right to education, a right to being looked after and a right to play. For a moment the place was absolutely still. I wasn't sure how the king was going to react and everyone was looking at him for a response. Because I couldn't understand his oral response, I watched his body language, which suggested that his reply to the children was measured and unemotional. Heather and Caroline later told me that the king had congratulated the children on their presentation but made no real commitment to them.

Marie-Joséphine and Roméo had asked me to hold a running session for all the RTP employees at the Cotonou office. Each week, on the Wednesday morning, they told me, the staff members do an exercise routine on the roof of the building. They wanted to add a "learn to run" session. Robert, Caroline, Heather and I arrived early at the office that Wednesday, and the first thing I did was give them a Running 101 tutorial. We chatted about shoes, hydration and nutrition, and then we hit the crazy streets of Cotonou.

The plan was to walk four minutes and run one minute, for 30 minutes. In Calgary, when you get to a crossing, the motorists are very good and stop for you. This was not Calgary. Fortunately we all survived the 2.62 km run and lived to run another day. Roméo and Mary-Joséphine told me that their objective was to run once a week and hit 5 km by week 12. I made Roméo club captain; he told me he would send a weekly report. And he did, while the club was still running.

We had two activities planned for the rest of the day. The first was tree planting. After cooling down and consuming several bottles of water, it was off to Houekegbo School and Tree Day. Tree Day is recognized throughout Benin. Deforestation has negatively affected Benin's water table and hence its ability to produce crops. Tree Day is a tangible celebration of the country's reforestation program, which has become a source of income for seedling producers and potentially for farmers as the country's soil improves. After we arrived and participated in an RTP game, we dug holes and planted 20 trees around the perimeter of the play area. After saying goodbye to the kids, we made our way to our next destination: Fidjrosse sports field.

There, we were to meet members of the Benin women's soccer team, who particularly wanted to talk to Caroline and Heather about women in sport. Both of the Olympians did an amazing job talking to girls who were being treated as outcasts because they played sports. When we arrived, a practice session was already in progress. Afterward, while Heather and Caroline talked to the young women about their sports careers, I headed off and found a bunch of kids to have a kick-a-bout with. After 20 minutes I was soaked and I headed back to the group.

Roméo caught me up on events on the field and told me the soccer players had informed the Olympians that Beninese girls who participate in sports are treated as freaks. They were expected to be at home doing chores instead of following their athletic dreams. Even getting an education was seen as a luxury for girls past Grade 5. Caroline and Heather told them that they were leaders of tomorrow and that change would happen. As I listened to the interchange, I realized how brave these young women were.

Travelling with Caroline and Heather was a lot of fun. They helped me with my French and were so supportive of the children we met at the schools. When they asked me what I was planning to do after the Benin trip, I joked that I was thinking about trying to get on *Mantracker* with my buddy Roy. *Mantracker*, of course, is the Canadian reality show featuring Terry Grant, the "Mantracker," who must chase two people in remote Canadian or American landscapes. These two people are called "prey," and their job is to evade capture even as they try to reach a finish line within 36 hours. I had first heard about the show through some kids I had met during Marathon Quest 250.

It just so happens that *Mantracker* is one of Caroline and Heather's favourite shows, and they offered to do a video, in support of Roy and me becoming "prey." I figured if we couldn't get on with the support of two Olympic gold medallists, then we were probably out of luck!

The day after our time with the women soccer players, we would learn a small part of Benin's history, which would have a profound impact on me. First, we travelled to Ouidah, 40 km west of Cotonou, and visited Adjara-Dovie Elementary School. We observed a lesson on child protection strategies. Right To Play recognizes that providing a child with a chance to play is only half the battle: kids cannot play and learn effectively if they do not feel safe. Child protection is a critical part of Right To Play's work. During the lesson, the children talked about their rights. These included the right to be taken seriously and the right to be safe at home. Each child stood up and gave an example. The children were in Grade 5 and were hard workers. The lesson was an hour long, and they stayed on task the whole time.

Our next stop was the Ouidah Museum, where we learned the story of the slave trade in Benin. In the 1700s, kings ruled the country, and they sold their own people to slave traders. A clay pipe was worth 20 slaves, and 50 fetched a bottle of gin. The slaves were kept for up to two months at the location that is now the museum. Many died before having to walk the 5 km trek along the slaves road to the coast, where they would board ships that would take them away. We drove that road, and along the way we were shown the slaves' graveyard, where millions are buried. At the end of the road we reached the "Port of No Return." The slaves would walk under an arch here, knowing they would never see their homeland again.

Slaves from what is now Benin and Togo were sent all over the world from this port, and half of them would die in the ships, never seeing land again. Standing on the beach, looking out to sea, I could only think, "But for the grace of God…"

It was hard to shake the imagery that had lodged in my mind after visiting Ouidah, but our journey to Benin was short and we didn't have time for silent contemplation that day. That evening, we headed over to Benin TV to participate in a one-hour program on the importance of sport in children's development. This was a national show broadcast across the country. The main speakers were Caroline and Heather, alongside Marie-Joséphine from Right To Play and a government representative. Robert and I sat in the back row behind the main speakers, with two members of the women's soccer team we had met the previous day. I really couldn't understand a lot of what was said, but it was obvious that the discussion was somewhat heated at times. I found out afterward that the presenter had been quite aggressive, asking why girls should participate in sports at all and demanding to know if there was any benefit to them. Interesting.

After the sombre day at Ouidah and the argumentative TV show, we had only two days left before our trip to Benin was over. Robert, Caroline, Heather and I had already visited a number of schools that used Right To Play programs, but our next visit would be extra special.

On the Friday, we made our way through the crazy Cotonou morning traffic and arrived at Vedoko School for the Deaf. The school had 120 students, many of whom were wearing Right To Play shirts. The school had three teachers, and the classrooms were on either side of a yard, at one end of which was an outdoor kitchen. Just as we arrived, the heavens opened and the rain came down. We were in Benin during the rainy season, but thus far we had been pretty lucky. We ran through the rain to a classroom, where we were welcomed by the head teacher and asked to present ourselves. Heather knows how to sign, and she explained she was a bobsledder and rugby player. Caroline demonstrated hockey and the teacher explained ice. I took advantage of the blackboard and drew a stick man and wrote 10,500 km next to him. I then drew a picture of Africa and a stick man on a bike and showed the Tour d'Afrique cycling route. The kids laughed their heads off at my diagrams, but I think they got the message.

Before we played a game from the RTP program, I headed outside. There was a lot going on and I just needed a moment to look around and take in the scene. The rain hadn't eased up, and part of the yard was flooding. Down the street I could see water creeping into the tin-roofed shops. There was no drainage system in the area, and the water carved a path along the road. This made me sad and somewhat dismayed. Here, they didn't even have basic drainage: when it rains, the shops and homes flood. Back in Canada, we moan if the street isn't immediately cleared of snow the morning after a dump.

When I returned to the class, we played some games, the first of which was a three-legged race. My partner was a Grade 1 student, Joseph. I didn't want to step on his toes so we went slowly. After the game, the teacher signed to the kids the importance of working together. We then did some balance games and team games. The kids couldn't get enough of these activities, and after each one the teacher would ask them to reflect on what they had learned. Soon it was time to go, and we bade another farewell.

Saturday was a big day for me. Not only was it my last day in Benin but also I was scheduled to lead a marathon for a group of kids. The farthest I had run in Benin so far was 2.6 km, so doing a marathon just a week after the Comrades and in 30° heat and 90 per cent humidity seemed a monumental task. Arriving at the CEGI sports field, I spotted 25 runners, all wearing numbers. I was

Enjoying a short run with members of the "Undefeatables" running club.

introduced to all the children and youth. Their leader was 26-year-old Parfaite, a member of the Benin women's soccer team. I asked about the marathon, and she said that 30 minutes of running would be enough. I must say, I was relieved!

We ran around the sports field a couple of times then headed out onto the streets of Cotonou. Again, I experienced the challenge of running in this city. The motorists and motorcyclists just weren't used to runners, especially girls, and a few of them shouted at us. After 30 minutes we'd covered 4.5 km, and everyone was back at the sports field safe and sound. Parfaite said that the group wanted to start a running club, so I asked her what it would be named. She went over to the group and they discussed my question. Five minutes later, she returned. She said they wanted to be called the "Undefeatables."

Undefeatables. That word pretty much summed up my feelings after five days in Benin. The kids I had met just want to be given a chance. They didn't want charity or pity. They wanted encouragement and support. For the first time, I saw with my own eyes how Right To Play was providing that helping hand, and I returned to Canada to continue supporting their good work.

I had found my new "normal," to carry on fundraising for Right To Play. Now I just needed to flesh out my plan.

Afterword

*"Setting an example is not the main means of
influencing another, it is the only means."*

—ALBERT EINSTEIN

When I returned from Benin in June, life didn't slow down. A
week later, I ran a half-marathon at Footstock in Cochrane, which
helped me get over jet lag and culture shock. The month continued
with a trip to Toronto for a presentation on Marathon Quest 250 at
the IdeaCity11 conference, then back to Canmore, Alberta, for the
Red Ball Golf tournament; one of RTP's bigger fundraising events.

By the time July came around, it was time for a break. Sue and I
headed over to England. We had decided to sell Sue's old house in
Dorset, as our son Calum was heading up to London. It made sense
for him to relocate, as he works in the film industry. It was quite an
emotional time for both Sue and Calum. He had lived most of his
life in that house, and Sue always loved going back there, especially
because it is walking distance from the beach and ocean.

Another reason it was important for us to go to England at this
time was to visit my sister Jan. She had been very sick with cancer
of the esophagus, and the chemo sessions were taking their toll.
During one afternoon I will always remember, Sue, Jan and I ate
ice cream on Bournemouth pier. It was great to be together again.
It was Jan who had introduced me to Sue back in 2003. As I write
this, I can look up and see a photo of us tucking into our cones that
day, enjoying the sunshine and sea view.

We had a chance to catch up with other relatives and some of
Sue's old friends. We even went back to the school where she used
to teach and enjoyed a Grade 2 concert. But the real highlight of
the trip was to be with Sue's mum, Terryanne, as she celebrated her
80th birthday. She and her husband, Eric, have been really supportive. We send them all the newspaper clippings covering my

quests, and Terryanne refers to me as "The Brit with Grit." I love them both dearly.

August came around and I had to make a trip to Toronto. On the flight back I had four hours to sit quietly and think. Sue met me at the airport and I told her, "I've had an idea." Of course, the last time I'd said that, she had sent me to the doctor. This time, I told her I had finally figured out how I was going to attempt to raise $1-million for RTP. I explained that I wanted to do 10 quests in five years in order to help 20,000 children and call it Quests for Kids. My trip to Benin had solidified my desire to continue supporting Right To Play, and my introduction to netball had sown the seed of an idea as to how that might be accomplished, through the quests.

I told Sue I would have certain criteria for the quests. Each quest must:

- include a sport that children can play at school or in the local community;
- be one of the following:
    - an attempt to set or break the Guinness World Record for the longest time played in that sport in one continuous match or game,
    - an attempt to set or break the Guinness World Record for the most players in an exhibition match or game of that sport, or
    - an extreme endurance event(s) in a particular sport;
- encourage children to become active and participate in sport; and
- be a fundraiser for Right To Play.

Marathon Quest 250 would count as the first quest in the series, and Netball Quest 61 would be the second. Sue was behind me, again, 100 per cent.

As August progressed, the pressure of organizing Netball Quest 61 began to build. By the beginning of September, we had only two weeks to put the finishing touches on the organization of the event. We only had 19 of the 24 players needed. The cost of the facility was $5,000 and the videography $4,000. So far we'd raised $1,000. Julie from Netball Alberta was pushing to get volunteers, and we still needed food suppliers to help out with meals. The one bright spot was Pablo from Radio Canada International, who wanted to set up a webpage about Quests for Kids.

A week before the game, things were falling into place. We had held a practice session and got to meet all the players for the first time. Eight were male, 16 female. Twelve were Senior A players with Netball Alberta, five were Senior B, and seven had very little or no experience. The countries the players originated from included Canada, England, Fiji, Australia, South Africa, New Zealand and Tanzania. A number of the players had represented Canada at the international level. Several are elite athletes and media personalities. They included Pete Estabrooks, one of Canada's pre-eminent fitness trainers; Christina Smith, bobsleigh Olympian; Lawrence Mafuru, owner of Boma Africa, a Kilimanjaro trekking company; and Buzz Bishop, social-media guru.

At 5.30 p.m. on Friday, September 16, two teams faced off at the South Fish Creek Recreational Complex, in Calgary's southeast. It was a gruelling 61 hours of play. We worked in shifts, with short meal and sleep breaks in between. The players were amazing and managed to get through the ordeal with only a couple of minor injuries.

At 5:30 a.m. on Monday morning, a huge cheer went up as the old record was beaten, and one hour later the 61-hour mark had been reached. There were a lot of tears and hugs. People who hadn't known one another a week ago had undertaken a challenge that would bond them for life. We thanked our many volunteers for their valuable contributions and headed outside for the first time in three days.

I drove home that morning feeling tired but euphoric. Little did I know, my good feelings would be gone in 30 minutes. My sister Jan had been moved to a hospice in early September, so I had booked flights to go and see her, planning to head out on September 21. As I arrived home after Netball Quest on that morning of September 19, Sue was waiting for me. She had reached home a short while before me and was there to take a call from England. As I got out of the car, I looked up at her and knew that Jan was gone.

My brother Pete and I headed over to England as planned. We spent time with Sally, Louise and Andrew and attended Jan's funeral with her husband, children and many friends.

When I returned, Sue and I felt we needed a holiday. We decided on a road trip. In the past, we have travelled by car west to Tofino on Vancouver Island, and north to Yellowknife. This year, we headed east for two weeks and visited the Maritimes. We flew to Halifax, having booked only our first and last nights' accommodations and leaving the rest up to fate. Our plan was to tour three of the Atlantic provinces: Nova Scotia, New Brunswick and Prince Edward Island.

Road trips always bring surprises. One of ours was hearing about the Prince Edward Island Marathon. I heard about it on the Wednesday and the race was on the Sunday. I really didn't have much time to think. We reached Charlottetown on the Saturday at 6:45 p.m. and I signed up.

On the Sunday morning, as I was waiting in the dark for the race bus, I saw a familiar face: my early-days mentor Vince from the Sudbury Rocks Running Club. He had coached me through my first two marathons and helped me qualify for Boston. He too was on a road trip and was running two marathons along the away.

The PEI Marathon is a point to point. The race starts at beautiful Brackley Beach in the famous Prince Edward Island National Park, on the north shore of the island. The start line is on the west side of the Brackley Beach change facilities, and marathoners proceed to the east, along the Gulf Shore Parkway, toward Dalvay.

I soon got into a good rhythm, and at every aid station I'd stop and chat with the volunteers. The first half of the race was along the ocean and then we headed inland along part of the Trans Canada Trail. Approaching the halfway point, I looked up the road, with the sun shining directly into my eyes, and was shocked to see the silhouette of a 6 m beaver. Another runner told me that this beaver (a plastic blow-up) travels to a lot of marathons.

At the 32 km mark I heard a yell: "Martin!" and three runners dressed as Anne of Green Gables caught me up. One was Cathy, with whom I had run the Comrades Marathon in South Africa that May. The running community is a small world. The "Annes" went ahead of me, and I came in at 4:44:17. As I crossed the line, the announcer mentioned I had run 250 marathons in 2010 for Right To Play. How did he know? I later found out that Sue had spilled the beans.

Rejuvenated from the trip out east, we returned home and started planning the quests in earnest. I wanted to set up three for 2012 – the third, fourth and fifth events in the series – and the preliminary work on them needed to be done before year end. I already knew that the third event in the quest series would be Lacrosse Quest 24. Scott, a lacrosse player, was part of the Netball Quest 61 team. During the 61 hours we had been on and off the court, he had told me about his love of lacrosse.

Scott and his brother Shawn run a company called Hotbox Lacrosse, which sells lacrosse apparel. He said they would be interested in working with me on a Guinness World Record for the longest game of Box Lacrosse. I contacted Guinness in London and found out that such a record had never been set, and that a minimum of 24 hours would have to be played in order to set one. I told Scott I had never played lacrosse but was keen to learn. We scheduled Lacrosse Quest 24 for April 27 and 28, 2012.

It seems that when you begin a quest, everything soon starts to fall into place.

One of Netball Quest 61's sponsors was a Calgary-based travel company called Downunder Travel. Its owner, Jason, told me he had an idea he wanted to discuss. At his office in Calgary, he told me about a 32 km race that takes place every year around the island of Rarotonga, in the Cook Islands. Jason had bought the rights to the race. His plan was to take me and 20 other interested parties down to the islands for a week or two, where we would do the main race plus some other smaller runs, and each person would raise money for Right To Play. He wanted to know if I would make it one of my quests for 2012. I thought about it for a few minutes and said, "For it to be a quest I would have to run three times around the island, in fact, let's just round up to a nice 100 km." And so Cook Islands Quest 100 was born and is scheduled for September 21 and 22, 2012.

The plans were being laid down quickly, but I still needed one more quest for 2012 and decided five-a-side soccer would be a good addition. I contacted Robin, the facility manager at Spray Lake Sawmills Family Sport Centre, as well as Lucy of the Cochrane Rangers, Allison at Cochrane Minor Soccer and Cynthia, the event coordinator at the sport centre. At around that time, I received this e-mail:

Hi Martin,
You probably don't remember me but I'm Nick Edwards, and I read your article in the Cochrane Times *about the world record for soccer. I play soccer for Cochrane Minor Soccer and love to play soccer on a regular basis and watch Arsenal on TV all the time, so when I saw your article in the paper, I got really excited. I would love to be a part of it, and if you haven't already decided who will be playing, I would love to play in your world-record-breaker.*
Hope I could play, thanks,
Nick Edwards

Nick was 12 years old at the time and so too young to participate as a player in the record-breaking attempt, but I made him part of the organizing committee. The first meeting went well, and we set October 5–7, 2012, for Soccer Quest 42: 42 hours of five-a-side soccer!

The year 2011 was ending as I wrapped up the scheduling for 2012's quests. One last event rounded out an interesting year: the Second Annual Marathon Quest Run–Walk. The event was held at the Spray Lake facility, and the marathon group headed off at 9:00 a.m. During the rest of the day, runners joined us for the half-marathon and for 10, 5 and 2.5 km runs, and by 3:00 p.m. the marathon was complete. In total we had 107 participants and raised $2,827, giving 140 kids a Right To Play program for one year.

As the New Year dawned, I was ready to tackle the events I had planned and more. I continued working with kids, now in a more official capacity. In the fall of 2011 I had signed up as a substitute resource assistant for the Rocky View Schools Division. I've very much enjoyed working with the kids and giving help wherever possible. I have no problems with quadratic equations, the periodic table or the history of the First World War, but a Grade 3 adverb–verb linking exercise gave me a bit of trouble in February!

As I write this in July 2012, I am still recovering from Lacrosse Quest 24. A group of 42 of us completed our goal of playing 24 hours of lacrosse, and Guinness has since verified our world record. I continue to schedule events for 2013. The sixth quest idea came to me in January when I participated again in the Kimmett Cup pond hockey tournament. During the game, I had a chance to chat with Reid Kimmett. He mentioned that he wanted to make the Fifth Annual Kimmett Cup in 2013 a memorable event and was thinking about setting a Guinness World Record for the most hockey players to participate in a game.

The inspiration for quest number seven came from my good friend Lawrence Mafuru, who lives in Canada and has a Mount Kilimanjaro trekking company called Boma Africa. He has climbed Kilimanjaro over 200 times. Lawrence and his wife, Leesha, have honoured me by asking me to be godfather to their baby girl, Oasis.

I will be heading to Tanzania in spring of next year for her naming ceremony. It just so happens that this will coincide with the Kilimanjaro Marathon, which I have decided to run. Combining this with a 24-hour climb to the summit will create Kilimanjaro Quest 95.2.

My eighth quest has to do with my friend Aaron McConnell, co-owner of a company called TransRockies Events, which runs seven bike and trail-running races in western Canada and the US. Aaron and I decided that completing all seven races in four months would be a great challenge as quest number 8. Time to dust off the bike.

That's the story so far. I still have to come up with ideas for quests nine and ten. Any suggestions?

Acknowledgements

I would like to recognize the following people for their help along the way.

Thanks, first, to my wife, Sue. We met at a New Year's party in 2003, and she's had to put up with my crazy ideas ever since. Over the years, she's turned up, in the early hours of the morning, at numerous ultra race check points, supplying me with chicken soup and ham sandwiches. She has believed in me from day one, and her faith never wavers.

I would like to thank my children, Kyle, Calum and Kristina, who supported me 100 per cent through all my adventures. My granddaughter, Autumn, who ran with me in Ontario, has kept all of her papa's newspaper clippings and has been as excited as anyone about my journey.

Marathon Quest 250 could never have taken place without the help of a group of dedicated people. Tom Healy introduced me to Right To Play and was a driving force behind Kids-U-Can. Jeffery Priebe developed the Marathon Quest 250 website; Lyn Cadence was my social media guru; and Cyrus Ameli and Tobi McLeod provided pictures and videography. Thanks, team!

Thanks to my medical–monitoring team – including family physician Dr. Bill Hanlon, physiotherapist Serge Tessier, chiropractor Greg Long, nutritionist Andrea Lympany, mental trainer Lisa Benz and data analyst Ross Stirling – I stayed on the road, physically and mentally, throughout the year.

Thank you, Robert Witchel and Sarah Stern at Right To Play. Robert and Sarah supported me all the way and allowed me the honour of visiting the children we helped in Benin, West Africa.

Thank you, Don Gorman and Neil Wedin at Rocky Mountain Books, and my editor Meaghan Craven, who helped turn a story into a book.

Community has been an important part of my journey. The running community is always giving, and I want to thank Andrew

Serle, Dean Karnazes, Bart Yasso, Ray Zahab and Ferg Hawk for their advice and support. Thanks also to members of the Cochrane Red Rock Running & Tri Club who would turn up and run with me when I least expected it. And thank you, Cochrane, Alberta, whose community came to my aid throughout the year.

I would also like to thank the many sponsors who helped me achieve my goal. I received gifts of shoes, clothes, flight tickets, hotel rooms, energy fuel, massages and hand warmers.

Finally, thanks go out to the many, many donors to Marathon Quest 250 and Right To Play, most of whom I haven't actually met! Thank you for having faith in me and my endeavours. Some of you I did meet, of course, most notably the children who ran with me on one of my 60 marathons at local schools. Children from all grades would come up to me as we ran around their sports fields, give me their pocket money and say, "This is to help the other children." Thank you.

A poster at Thorncliffe School shows children cheering "Marathon Martin" as he completes one of his 250 marathons.